The Dawn of the New Creation

Exploring the Christian Hope As Told by Revelation

Brayden Rockne Brookshier

"When people think of revelation, they often mistakenly think only of judgment and the destruction of the world. This book, *The Dawn of the New Creation*, captures the true essence, the new world, and reality God is preparing for his people. I recommend strongly not just reading but meditating on the themes uncovered in this excellent work. In actuality, we are citizens of heaven/the New Creation, and this will help us realize our wondrous present as well as our glorious future. Our lives will be changed, and we will see everything a lot more clearly as a result. It is exciting to see this extremely positive work on the Apocalypse come to light."

—Grant R. Osborne, author of *Revelation: Verse by Verse* & *The Hermeneutical Spiral*

"In this extremely well written piece, Brayden Brookshier effectively identifies common misunderstandings concerning redemptive history, while directing the reader to a more biblically precise way of discussing the major themes of Revelation. Brookshier's use of both creative illustrations and scholarly analysis makes *The Dawn of the New Creation* an absolute must-read for anyone seeking greater clarity regarding the eternal hope promised to those in Christ Jesus."

—J. D. Eldridge, President, Branch College

"I've been reading and studying Apocalyptic literature all my life. It's been decades since I've read a book on Revelation that captured my imagination. Brayden Brookshier in his book *The Dawn of the New Creation* not only challenged my thinking but presented some fresh ideas that pushed me out of my proverbial box and beyond! I loved his take on "heavenizing earth."

Frankly, the majority of scholarly works I've read on Revelation leave me feeling guilty. Guilty for yearning for some version of heaven that feels a little like my home, planet earth. Brayden applied scholarly exegesis to Revelation and the results are exciting. I hope you will take the time to read *The Dawn of the New Creation*. I promise you won't feel guilty but rather exhilarated about heaven, earth, and a glorious future!"

—Steve Bombaci, Pastor, Newbreak Church Pacific Beach

"Ever find yourself a bit fearful of the Book of Revelation—or a bit too nonchalant about what it actually means for your life? Then let me introduce you to Brayden Brookshier, who unveils a treasure trove of truths about the final book of the Bible. These aren't just nuggets, folks. These insights are the kind that should have followers of Christ everywhere both lifting our hands in awesome wonder and bowing in the [face] of such beautiful hope.

After reading this book, I'm convinced you'll see Revelation in an entirely new light and start to think of the last book of the Bible as the bridge to a new book—a living book in which you're one of the characters—that's far better than you've ever dared to imagine."

—Caleb Breakey, author of *Sermon Crunch: Write a Powerful Sermon in Half the Time*

To King Jesus—may this book exalt your name and celebrate your incomprehensible grace. This book is a response to wondering at your love. My hope is to tell the world of who you are, what you have done, and what you will do.

To Ariana, my bride—you have always supported me. Through high and low points, you never let me forget God's call on our lives as a team. I am forever grateful for your love and support. Thank you for being my loving companion in the adventure so far, with so much more ahead.

To the staff at the Branch College, friends and mentors alike—Wayne Kinde, Brooks Fuller, J. D. Eldridge, Sean Henschel, Matt Marzec, and Richard Cates, you all have inspired me and play a pivotal role in my personal growth and passion for faithful exegesis.

To Caleb Breakey and Adam Swiger, who have helped this project become even greater than I thought possible—a simple thank you cannot suffice in conveying my gratitude.

To my readers—I wrote this for you. If your life has been blessed because of this book, then that is a win for my years of effort. You, my readers, are what propels me toward future projects. Thank you for allowing me to play a part in inspiring your story and testimony.

CONTENTS

The Most Extraordinary Letter 3

A Tale of Two Trees 15

The Emerald Throne 29

The Scroll of Salvation 55

The Coronation of Heaven's King 73

The Wedding of Two Worlds 103

God's Thesis Statement 127

The Most Holy Place 151

The World Created for the Son 181

The End Is the New Beginning 215

Notes 227

About the Author 249

About Sermon To Book 251

The Most Extraordinary Letter

And the seventh angel blew the trumpet, and there was a loud voice in heaven saying, "The kingdom of the world has become the kingdom of our Lord and of his Christ, and he will reign forever and ever."

—Revelation 11:15

Revelation is the most extraordinary book of the Bible—both literally and literarily! This circular letter is written in a genre completely foreign to the modern world. We simply do not have modern writings quite like apocalyptic prophecy.

Most likely written sometime during the last decade of the first century, Revelation is the final book of the biblical canon and was written by the last living apostle—John. In studying this book, it is impossible to leave out the discussion of eschatology, which is the study of last, final, or ultimate things. Because Revelation talks about the end of human history as we know it and the beginning of the new world, it is appropriate for Revelation to be the last book of God's Word.

The Apocalypse

Revelation 1:1 begins with the "apocalypse" of Jesus Christ. *Apocalypse*, in the original Greek, literally means "revelation." It is an unveiling of something previously not known. What exactly is being revealed? Jesus Christ is, but also "what must soon take place" (Revelation 1:2) is being declared.

At the time Revelation was written, Jewish expectation anticipated God making all things right and establishing "new heavens and a new earth" (Isaiah 65:17; 66:22). So, there were answers to the "what"—a new creation—and the "why"—that is, to have eternal life with God and other believers in a redeemed cosmos; however, the "how" has always been a point of ambiguous contention.[1]

The major plot of Revelation is the unveiled plan of God's kingdom coming to transform all of creation. It reveals how God is bringing redemptive history to its consummate state of glory because of the victorious work of Christ—who has become the King of heaven and earth—and will one day bring His kingdom reality to all the cosmos.

New Creation as a Biblical Lens for Revelation

Growing up, I heard a lot of sermons about "heaven."[2] Between the church camps, altar calls, and small groups, "heaven" was a lighthearted topic of hope and joy. As I began to read the Bible and grow in my knowledge of God's Word, however, I noticed something. The more common, western concept of "heaven" didn't exactly line up with what the Bible taught.

The idea that when we die our highest hope is to float away to heaven—which is what I had always heard—wasn't making sense, biblically. It's not that a different gospel was being preached, but certainly a wrong notion of our eternal hope. I began to become passionate about this topic and vigorously study it to see what the Bible truly has to say about "heaven." The desire to know God's Word—and what it says about our great salvation—is the very inspiration behind the writing of this book.

I believe all of our talk about "heaven" is more precisely a conversation about new creation. The concept of "new creation" is a dominant theme in the biblical narrative. This single eschatological lens can unlock so many rich treasures to understanding the intention of the redemptive drama.

More specifically, Revelation is a deep book, so I am going to take the approach of honing in on the lens of "new creation," so that we can see how two major key movements of the book reveal this ultimate biblical goal, which has been anticipated ever since Genesis 1:1.

In light of this, the entire Bible is eschatological; the whole story encompasses the cumulative journey toward new creation as the purpose and goal of the biblical plotline. It can even be said that new creation has been central to the ancient Jewish hope all along.[3]

Our True Eternal Hope

Interestingly, in Revelation, the word for "heaven," *ouranos*, is never used to describe the final state of believers. It is used either of the present dwelling of God or of the physical starry expanse. So, you will see me propose returning to more biblically accurate language to talk about our eternal hope.

As Christians, how can we tell others about our glorious salvation if we don't even know what the Bible says about the destiny of creation? In this book, I hope to give you a chance to fall in love again with the doctrine of eschatology.

Many average Christians reserve this subject for the academically trained or spiritually elite. I suggest that the lens of new creation not only unlocks ancient treasures in the Bible, but also helps our hearts live more profoundly in the present, alive to the wonder of God's redemptive work, which has begun in the present but will culminate in the future.

My hope for this book is that it would provide you with a biblical foundation for the utmost confidence and celebration of your eternal hope as a Christian. If it is grounded in Scripture, hope is not some flippant wish that may or may not happen. Hope that is rooted in the Bible gives us an unwavering confidence. And hope is something we all need. As believers, we need hope to endure. And the person who is not a Christian needs hope to find the true purpose of life. This book is all about how the new creation, specifically in Revelation, gives us a hope that makes our hearts full of bounding joy that will compel us to give our lives to sharing this hope with everyone that we possibly can.

Five Key Movements

In my studies of Revelation, I have found five explicit and preeminent key movements that will culminate in new creation: exhortation to the churches (chapters 1–3), the throne room vision (chapters 4–5), judgment administered (chapters 6–18), eschatological salvation (chapters 19–20), and the new creation (chapters 21–22).

All of these point toward the unveiling of the exalted Christ and His sovereignty over human history. Thus, Revelation is supremely theological and theocentric, highlighting the triune God as the center of all things. Our focus will be in examining two key movements: the throne room vision (Revelation 4–5) and the new creation (Revelation 21–22).

A Note on the Genre of Revelation

World-renowned New Testament scholar Grant Osborne suggests an important note on apocalyptic symbolism: "Those who take it as completely literal miss the very nature of the apocalyptic genre, yet to take it as entirely symbolic misses the mark as well. In Jewish apocalyptic literature, the two aspects are blended and interdependent, and each symbol must guide us as it functions in its context."[4]

That presents us with a challenge when parsing this text. We cannot over-spiritualize it, making everything symbolic; however, we can't read this as literally as we would read the newspaper, either. We cannot read this book like we read other books of the Bible. We must read it as an apocalyptic prophecy functioning as a letter of exhortation to real churches in the latter part of the first century.

Revelation is not a roadmap about the end of the world. Revelation is not a puzzle that requires decoding. Although John uses vivid symbolism, the symbols can be interpreted through an understanding of the ancient world and the study of Scripture that was written prior to Revelation.

The task of the modern reader is to look at the text with ancient eyes. Everything I present here, while having modern relevance, is rooted in faithful interpretation of the history and grammar of the Scriptures being examined.

Key Terms Defined

Here are some key terms that may require a brief explanation so that you can follow along with clarity:

- **The Fall**—the detrimental moment in Genesis 3 when Adam and Eve rebelled against God after being lured into sin by Satan. Their choice brought not only sin, but all the physical and spiritual consequences of sin into the world.

- **Trinity/Triune**—the word that encapsulates God's nature being three distinct persons (Father, Son, and Holy Spirit) but one eternal deity. Because Scripture usually speaks of "God" as specifically God the Father, it is helpful to use the terminology found in Ephesians 4, namely that is there is one God (the Father), one Lord (Jesus Christ), and one Spirit (the Holy Spirit), which are distinct in person but one in essence.

- **Salvation**—God's rescue or deliverance of His people. In the Old Testament, the Exodus was the dominant salvific event; in the New Testament, it is the cross. By trusting in Jesus, people are rescued from sin's penalty and power and saved for God's glory. Upon trusting in the Lord Jesus, individuals receive the Holy Spirit as a gift to guide them and transform their lives.

- **Eschatology**—that which is concerned with the study of last, final, or ultimate things. It is not always limited to the talk of chronological "last" things, but it can also be speaking of the ultimate fulfillment of the intended purpose of something. This can be used as an adjective, "eschatological," to dress up a certain word, describing it with ultimacy.

- **Inaugurated Eschatology**—that which has begun and is true now. While it may be awaiting a greater fulfillment, much of Christian eschatology has an "already/not yet" paradoxical tension. God's redemptive work is initiated but has not culminated. Synonyms include *initiated*, *commenced*, and *launched*.

- **Future Eschatology**—that which will be fulfilled in the future; something that has not happened yet. For example, the ushering in of the "new heavens and new earth" simply has not taken place for anyone yet; that is anticipated in the future. Typically, in biblical eschatology, it is important to maintain that the confidence of certainty of something coming to fruition is grounded in God's promise to make it so.

• **Eschaton**—Greek for "end" or "last," referring to the return of Christ and the end of history.[5] It is a word pregnant with meaning, alluding to the end and ultimate culmination of God's sovereign plan. This includes the return of Christ and the final judgment when God will eradicate the world of sin, death, decay, etc., and usher in the new heavens and the new earth.

• **Heaven**—a confusing term because of what people have made it to mean. In biblical literature, heaven can simply mean the starry expanse visible above us. It can mean God's abode in a dimension different from our own. Believers who have passed on and are with the Lord right now are in "heaven" in the sense that they are in God's abode and presence. In modern theology, the term heaven seems to signify the eternal state, but that has always seemed strange to me. I would prefer to call the eternal state such things as "the new heavens and new earth," "the new earth," "the new world," "the new creation," or "the eternal state."

• **The Intermediate State/Afterlife**—sometimes referred to as "paradise" in biblical literature;

this is the place where people go in between the present and the future coming of Christ. The intermediate state is not the final destination for people. Our immediate "afterlife" as Christians is not the culminate new creation with the new heavens and new earth. While individuals in paradise are filled with bliss, there is still a sense of waiting for the eternal state to come to pass. For the believer and the non-believer, it is a much different experience in different realms.

- **The Eternal State**—as this pertains to believers, it is the final, eternal dwelling place of God with His people, which will be perfect and unending. This is commonly spoken of as the subject of "heaven," and it contains the arrival of the new heavens and new earth and every blessing that comes to fruition with that change.

- **Jesus**—Jesus has many names/titles that can be the substantive for His name. In the book of Revelation, He is predominately referred to as the "Lamb." He is also the "Lion," which connects Him to the Lion of the tribe of Judah motif. Revelation also calls Jesus the "Alpha and the Omega" and the "King of kings and Lord of lords." However, some common biblical titles for Him include "Son of God"— emphasizing His ontological, royal identity as the prince of creation; "Christ/Messiah"— emphasizing His functional role as the promised Messianic Savior; "Lord"—taken from the same

Greek word that was translated "Yahweh" in the Old Testament, and which emphasizes His preexistence as the great I AM. This title is arguably the most explicit of Jesus' deity and identifies Him as the divine ruler of the cosmos and the King of His people.

Dare to Read On

If you are reading this, take heart. This book was written in such a way that a scholar could appreciate it, but it is also geared toward the lay Christian who is looking to learn more about the overarching theme of new creation in the Bible.

I encourage you to follow along with all Scripture passages that are being examined. Scripture passages in this text will come from the *Lexham English Bible* (LEB), unless specified differently (sometimes I prefer my own translation of the text upon examining the Greek).

I invite you to press forward in this endeavor, ready to meditate further on what you may already know and to learn things that you do not yet know. The workbook sections at the end of each chapter will help you internalize key truths as you work your way through this study.

Get ready to enter the world of biblical apocalyptic literature. Your imagination will be stimulated. Your convictions will be challenged. And your soul will be strengthened. I hope you are half as excited as I am! But first, before we dive in to the apocalypse, let us utilize a chapter that catches us up into a brief overview of the biblical drama demonstrating the need for God to make all things new.

CHAPTER ONE

A Tale of Two Trees

"Go back?" he thought. "No good at all! Go sideways? Impossible! Go forward? Only thing to do! On we go!"[6]
—**J. R. R. Tolkien's *The Hobbit***

Read: Genesis Chapters 1–3

I sat in my chair, probably the most unsettled individual in the whole room. "So, Jesus saves us," the preacher continued, "and takes us back to the garden of Eden." His sermon concluded rather poetically, and many people responded to his evangelistic message and came down to the altar. Ironically, I agreed with the vast majority of what was said in the sermon, but there was one thing that I remembered, the very thing that bothered me.

Most people have an overly romantic view of Eden as perfect. Now, we can acknowledge that Eden was very good. However, Eden was not a perfected and permanent state. Eden was not the eschaton. In other words, Eden was never mankind's final and highest state of potential—it was never our final destination. The original creation was always a signpost for the new creation. The pliable has to make way for the perfect.

There is a problem if we assume that "sinless" means "perfect." This is a crucial nuance we must be willing to embrace. If we communicate Eden as being "perfect," we have to defend Eden as the highest, pinnacle form of both human and cosmological existence. If anything can trump in excellence over Eden, then we admit that Eden, while very good, still had a progressive destiny.

Otherwise, if salvation is simply "returning to the garden" and the life of Adam and Eve before the Fall, how can we have assurance that we won't mess it all up again?

From the first pages of the Bible, it becomes apparent that God is working toward something more, something better, something new. New creation is the goal of the biblical narrative from even the first moment of creation.

No one, not even Adam, has lived in the final existence intended by God for mankind. You read that correctly. Even before the Fall, Eden needed a Messiah. As provocative as that sounds, it is biblically true. Not even Adam has seen life in its fullest potential.

Allow me to open your eyes to the Eden you never knew. It was a place of wonder but also warfare. A place that was sinless but not serpent-less. A place that had eschatological potential but was not ultimately perfected. Welcome to the jungle.

Guarding the Garden

When God breathed life into Adam, He created him

amid a cosmic construction site. While Eden was a flourishing garden, the surrounding world was chaotic and needed subduing. Adam was to be God's agent in making the rest of the world look like Eden. Mankind, made in the image of God (Genesis 1:26), was born with a mission.

One tree was put off-limits—the tree of knowledge of good and evil. One tree was put on probation—the tree of life. The tree of knowledge of good and evil was a sacrament of mankind's dependence on God. The tree of life was a sacrament of the higher form of life.

Eden was not a static state. It would be impossible for Adam and Eve's existence to continue in the way Eden had been created. God's original commission of Adam in Genesis 2:15 was to 'cultivate and keep' Eden. The call to cultivation implied nurturing and expanding Eden. The second word, 'keep,' is a very interesting word because it denotes the task of guarding or protecting something. Immediately, we realize Adam was placed in a trial, where an intruder threatened the current progress and the future potential of humanity and creation.

But who is this mysterious enemy? The serpent, who once fell from heaven, had come to taint God's good world. To inherit the tree of life, Adam had to slay the serpent and remain totally allegiant to God. The trajectory of creation hinged upon the outcome of Adam's leading.

But as we know, Adam and Eve were defeated by the serpent, not through combat but through deception. Their actions in eating of the prohibited tree of knowledge of good and evil demonstrated that their love for God lacked maturity, and the severity of their willful rebellion couldn't be more exaggerated.

Instead of looking to God alone to grow in the wisdom of untainted holiness and goodness, mankind took a fatal detour, looking to alternative routes, as if there were any other way besides God's way. Anything opposed to the path of life is a path of death, no matter how slight the deviation. Humanity deteriorates when it seeks autonomy apart from God—when all along we were meant to be creatures dependent on our Creator.

The First Sin

Adam, and thereby humanity's circumstances in the garden, present to us God's heart in establishing relationship with us: that of a willful choice of love. God did not create people to be emotionless, soulless robots. He could have programmed us like a computer to perform a specific set of functions, but that was not His choice.

We are made with the highest dignity imaginable, created in the very image and likeness of our Creator. So, God gave mankind the quintessential test of love. Through the unexplained and mysterious prohibition of the tree of knowledge of good and evil, God proposed a question of covenantal relationship to mankind: "Do you trust Me?"

Perhaps the oversimplification provided no favors. More accurately, God was demanding that Adam and Eve give Him their unrivaled allegiance. The premiere sin of mankind was not one of pride, selfishness, or ignorance. It couldn't have been a sinful desire to be like God, for mankind was already like God, made in His image (Genesis 1:26–27).

Ignorance wouldn't be able to vindicate our first parents, as they were instructed to not eat of that tree. God didn't need to give an explanation; He deserves our loyal trust despite our knowing, or not knowing, all the details.

The first sin is also the root of every other sin. It is the grave notion of thinking there is an alternative to absolute devotion to God alone. This is a step further than monotheistic worship; this is "God-onlyism."[7]

The moment when Adam and Eve sinned took place prior to the bite into the forbidden fruit. It was the moment the serpent cunningly led Adam and Eve to believe that total allegiance to God was not the *only* option.

Prior to the specifications of our sin, there is always the initial root of temptation that distracts our attention away from goodness and toward rebellion. All sin stems from entertaining the thought that there is another way other than the way of the Lord. As soon as we think there is another option, we are headed toward the destructive path of sin and away from the blessing. Perhaps this would be a good time to remind you that the original definition of sin is to "miss the mark."

Anything antagonistic to God's design (i.e., sin) screams through our actions that we not only think we know better than God, but that we love something more than Him.

A Place of Probation

Notice that Adam and Eve had not yet graduated from their probationary testing. They had not yet been awarded the privilege to eat of the tree of life, otherwise they would have obtained immortal life "and live[d] forever" (Genesis

3:22).

After the entrance of sin into the world, in Genesis 3:22–24, the tree of life was restricted, kept away from fallen man. The fruit of the tree of life could not be consumed by sinners. It would have been utterly disastrous for our first parents to achieve immortality in their sinful state.

The cosmology of Genesis 1–3 shows that Eden was a place of probation. The tree of life serves as a sacramental sign of the immortality and glory to be granted to mankind upon the condition of perfect obedience by which Adam failed.

This is where the enriching study of Jesus being the "Last Adam" pays dividends. It is only because Jesus was faithful as our covenant mediator that we can obtain eternal life and a right relationship with the triune God.

It is only in Christ that we can obtain the tree of life with all its blessings. Thus, in Jesus' letter to the church of Ephesus in Revelation 2, He offers believers who endure until the end the ability to obtain the tree of life as a reward. He is, in essence, offering eschatological life beyond probation, even beyond Eden.

Preconsummate Stage

The tree of life plays a pivotal role in biblical cosmology. It is a picture of vitality and freshness, without decay. We know that ultimately God is the Source of life, both creating life and sustaining it, but the tree of life is God's symbolic aesthetic to communicate this fact.

Not only does it communicate life unending, but the tree is a symbol of intimate accord with God. The tree shows us that man is totally dependent upon God, even in a sinless condition. At the Fall, when the tree of life was first restricted, Adam and Eve lost the potential of immortal life and the closeness in their relationship to God.

There would be some serious problems if we saw Eden as the culmination of God's design. We must not forget who and what was also in the garden. The serpent, Satan, was in the garden tempting Adam and Eve.

Perpetual conflict with the serpent is not the ideal state of mankind's eternal residence. Likewise, the presence of the tree of knowledge of good and evil, being prohibited with severe consequences, signifies the threat of death as hovering over Adam and Eve if they partook of the fruit of the tree.

We must remove the overly romanticized view of Eden as the perfect state and the final goal of man. Although Eden was sinless in its commencement, it was still incomplete; it still needed consummation.

It was "very good," and it had the eschatological potential to graduate to God's intended perfection—the new heavens and the new earth—but it did not get there. Sin derailed mankind from entering eternal glory and escalating all of creation, all of the cosmos, into eternal glory.

The pre-consummate stage in Eden still needed to reach the completed and irreversible stage. Consider these five primary conditions that needed to be dealt with before immortal life could be secured:

1. Victory over the presence of evil (by defeating the serpent and his followers).

2. Ultimate security against committing sin (the inner transformation of the heart and the removal of the probationary tree of knowledge of good and evil).

3. The receipt of immortality (by partaking of the tree of life and having union with the Source of life, God).

4. Protection from creation decaying (ushering in the new heavens and new earth, which will maintain a constant, fresh newness to them).

5. Consummation of the first marriage to transcend to its final form (between Christ and the Church).

The existence of these conditions does not undermine God's sovereignty. For reasons that are far beyond my comprehension—and not given explanation in the Bible—God is bringing mankind to the highest aim of new creation knowing that the Fall would be part of the process.

Ultimately, God is in control over all circumstances, and we see that, despite the pathway to get there, God is working all things toward the perfect eternal state. And that is what we will explore in the following chapters.

The Promised Eternal State

New creation has been the grand objective ever since the original creation. Genesis 1–2 present to us a project site, not a finished one. As N.T. Wright notes, "...even the glorious world of Genesis 1 was the beginning of something, rather than an end in itself. It was itself a great sign-post, pointing to the world that God always intended to make out of it."[8]

Our journey in studying the doctrine of new creation in the book of Revelation has begun with our acknowledgment of the need for new creation. There is no way to go backward; in fact, Eden was not meant to be the final destination.

We must move forward with our thinking to correspond with what God is sovereignly doing as He is ushering in the new creation through our inaugurated experience. We must also anticipate and have a biblical view of hope as we look forward to the future eschatological consummation of everything being made new in the promised eternal state.

In the words of Tolkien, "On we go!"

WORKBOOK

Chapter One Questions

Main Truth: The original creation is but a signpost pointing us to the coming reality of the new creation.

Question: When you hear the word *heaven*, what images and ideas come to mind? Are these based on scripture or on cultural ideas?

God + Jesus, Peace, happy
People, angels, always bright
+ Sunny, beautiful, glowing

Both

_____

_____

Question: Have you ever heard or read the idea of heaven as a return to Eden or an Edenic state? Why was Eden never able to be the perfect and final home for God and His people?

_Sort of_____

_____

We are not perfect. He
gave us free will to
choose.

_____

_____

_____

_____

_____

_____

_____

Question: How do we see that the new creation has been God's plan all along, even from the dawn of the old creation? How is the original creation a signpost that points to the new?

_____

_____

_____

_____

_____

_____

_____

_____

_____

_____

_____

_____

Action: Using a Bible concordance or software, research each mention of the "tree of life" in Scripture. List your findings and what they tell you about this amazing tree. We will look at it in more depth later in this book.

Symbolic meaning: a symbol of a fresh start on life, positive energy, good health, and a bright future.
As a symbol of immortality.

Genesis: The tree of the knowledge of good an evil which was planted in the Garden of Eden.

Chapter One Notes

_____

_____

_____

_____

_____

_____

_____

_____

_____

_____

_____

_____

_____

_____

_____

_____

_____

_____

_____

_____

_____

_____

CHAPTER TWO

The Emerald Throne

Worship is praise in response to God's revelation of himself.[9]

—Richard D. Phillips

Read: Revelation 4:1-8

If I were to knock on your door, you would probably answer it, and you might even invite me inside. Unless they are some big shots who have immense influence, most people don't have security protocol preventing others from knocking on their doors. We often have a doormat that says something along the lines of "welcome" when guests arrive at our doorstep.

Now, if I attempted to go to the White House and knock on the door, I wouldn't even be able to get close to the door without being intercepted by security. The president of the United States is not an individual whom we can go visit on our own prerogative. Only if we have an invitation can we meet with such a powerful person.

We begin with an obvious observation—no one can go knocking on the door to God's throne. Western Christianity has perhaps overemphasized God's accessibility with not much attention placed on His holy transcendence. Only by being summoned can someone, literally, come up to His presence.

Jesus Himself, in Revelation 4:1 ("the first voice"),[10] summons John to the throne room of God. The throne was always seen as the central focal point in Jewish thought. Being consistent with its roots, Revelation is structured to show the throne of God as a focal point of the book. The word *throne* is used a total of sixty-two times in the entire New Testament, and forty-seven of these occurrences are found in Revelation.

Behind the Scenes

In Revelation 4, John gets a look behind the scenes—the view from heaven despite the chaotic turmoil happening on earth. We get a glimpse of God's vantage point. Here we get to see God's throne room as it appears in the present condition, that is, "heaven" as it is at the moment.

The sporadic imagery is not meant to give us a tour of the room, but rather, it communicates something about God's majesty. This type of apocalyptic vision is not foreign to biblical literature. Isaiah 6, Ezekiel 1–2, and Daniel 7 bear resemblance.

This is no subtle vision. Revelation 4–5, as one cohesive scene, provides the interpretative key to understanding the totality of the book. Misunderstand these chapters, and you probably will misunderstand the book of Revelation as a whole.

John is taken to another dimension, it seems, to see a heavenly perspective that helps him, and his readers, understand what is happening on earth from a theocentric lens.

This is significant, because Revelation is an unveiling that guides the reader to understand past events, such as the death and resurrection of Jesus; present events, pertaining to the first-century audience; and future events, such as the return of Christ and the ushering in of the new heavens and the new earth—and how they all fit together.

John's vantage point is not as most people would think of it. It is not that heaven is somewhere far out among the stars and that John was teleported there. Most westerners have a wrong concept of heaven and earth. Heaven is typically viewed as the immaterial and spiritual, while the earth is the physical and generally has bad or evil connotations.

Many of our misconceptions come, primarily, from medieval theology and art. However, even John's original audience had enough dualistic misconceptions that needed correction.

The reality is that heaven and earth are intimately related and interlocked. Heaven and earth are separated by dimension, not galaxies. N.T. Wright helps us understand: "'Heaven,' God's sphere of reality, is right here, close beside us, intersecting with our ordinary reality. It is not so much like a door opening high up in the sky, far away. It is more like a door opening right in front of us where before we could only see this room, this field, this street."[11]

He goes on to say, "[John's vision] is about a prophet

being taken into God's throne room so that he can see 'behind the scenes' and understand both what is going to take place and how it all fits together and makes sense."[12]

World of Color

After these things I looked, and behold, an open door in heaven, and the former voice that I had heard like a trumpet speaking with me was saying, "Come up here and I will show you the things which must take place after these things."

Immediately I was in the Spirit, and behold, a throne was set in heaven, and one was seated on the throne. And the one seated was similar in appearance to jasper and carnelian stone, and a rainbow was around the throne similar in appearance to emerald.

—Revelation 4:1–3

When was the last time you were lost in wonder? When was the last time you were baffled beyond belief? Many would concur that we have lost our sense of imagination. Maybe the constant stimulation we have from all the technology accessible to us today has caused our brains to be less creative.

One thing I love about the Bible is its ability to help us reclaim what we have lost. Reading the book of Revelation is far from boring. For many it is confusing, yet intriguing. Understanding Revelation as it was meant to be understood is not only part of our due diligence in studying the Bible, but it also allows us to be as astonished as John was when he wrote what was unveiled to him. And that is precisely what happens as we look to chapters 4–5.

At Disneyland's California Adventure, there is one of

the most impressive attractions I have ever seen: World of Color. For over twenty minutes, a spectacular production is displayed for hundreds of viewers.

The water in the middle of the hub of California Adventure sprouts upward with various colors dancing to the music playing over the speakers. Clips of famous Disney movie scenes are played, and the lights, water, and even flames of fire correspond to the music.

It is easy to lose track of time when viewing such a spectacle. The vibrant colors are marvelous. The sights, the sounds, the whole experience is memorable for kids and adults alike.

As I study Revelation 4, I can't help but think of the World of Color experience at Disneyland. I can bet with confidence that God's throne room—with its colors, lights, sounds, and grandeur—is far superior to any production Disney can put on.

The description of God, the One seated on the throne, is vague. Instead of the normal details we would expect, we are told that John saw vibrant colors and bright lights. It is like John cannot find the language to describe the gorgeous majesty of God and His throne, so he uses a description of radiant, precious stones as the closest thing.

Two of the twelve stones that were to be on the high priest's breastplate were jasper and carnelian (Exodus 28:17–20). Evidently, the stones on the breastplate reflected God's own glory as the high priest wore it. Jasper is an opaque stone that could be red, green, or blue, or could have been a diamond. Carnelian is a fiery red stone.

The "rainbow" of light around the throne is God's emerald-colored headgear, reflecting His indescribable majesty. This description also lines up with the description of God found in Ezekiel 1:26–28, in which there is a world of color of glorious light proceeding from God's throne and presence.

This also agrees with Psalm 104:2, in which the psalmist acknowledges of God, "You cover Yourself with light" (GNT).[13] The Common English Bible (CEB) dynamically translates the Psalm, "You wear light like a robe." Again, the text draws our attention to a God so beautiful, so full of splendor, that He radiates magnificent light around Him. The closest comparison we can draw is imagining His emerald throne being like a throne encompassed by the aurora borealis—more commonly known as the 'northern lights.' How can we not be in awe of a God whose throne emulates such lavish light?

The ancient reader would have been drawn into the scene presented in this passage, as we all should be. God's glory is captivating. Not only is this true of His throne and physical appearance, but His character also captivates us. His royal beauty is accompanied by His royal goodness. He is a King who is worthy of worship.

I am reminded of "Beautiful," a song by music artist Phil Wickham that praises the beauty of God. I wish there were more songs like it. There cannot be too many songs written about God's attributes and actions, or His beauty and splendor.

The Throne Room

And around the throne were twenty-four thrones, and seated on the thrones were twenty-four elders dressed in white clothing, and on their heads were gold crowns. And from the throne came out lightnings and sounds and thunders, and seven torches of fire were burning before the throne, which are the seven spirits of God. And before the throne was something like a sea of glass, like crystal, and in the midst of the throne and around the throne were four living creatures full of eyes in front and in back. And the first living creature was similar to a lion, and the second living creature was similar to an ox, and the third living creature had a face like a man's, and the fourth living creature was similar to an eagle flying. And the four living creatures, each one of them, had six wings apiece, full of eyes around and inside, and they do not have rest day and night, saying,

"Holy, holy, holy is the Lord God All-Powerful, the one who was and the one who is and the one who is coming!
—Revelation 4:4–8

The earth revolves around the sun, not the other way around. In God's reality, everyone and everything revolves around Him. God is the central focal point of the heavenly throne room, and His throne is the center of the universe. All attention is solely on Him. There is nothing in the throne room worthy of worship other than God alone. Heaven truly is theocentric.

In this description of the throne room, we are introduced to twenty-four elders. According to Ronald Trail's commentary on Revelation, they represent the twelve tribes of Israel plus the twelve apostles, ultimately symbolizing the universal Church—the people of God spanning throughout the Old and New Testament, both Jews and Gentiles.[14]

The term for "elders" never applies to angels, which provides further evidence that these are redeemed people. And it makes sense for the crown of a conqueror to be given to believers rather than angels. In Revelation 2:10, the "crown of life" is offered as a reward to all believers who prevail.

In addition to this, they wear "white garments," which denote ritual purity, having been cleansed and forgiven of sin. After being washed in the blood of the Lamb, believers become pure and radiantly white (Revelation 7:14; 22:13–14). The twenty-four elders are redeemed people from both the Old and New Testament eras, and they now have begun to receive the rewards promised in the seven letters of Revelation 2 and 3.[15]

Out of the throne comes thunder and lightning. The atmospheric phenomena recall God's appearance at Mount Sinai in Exodus 19:16 in thunder and lightning and a thick cloud.[16] We must also note how this phenomenon moves the plot forward in Revelation.

At the end of the seventh seal, "There were peals of thunder, rumblings, flashes of lightning, and an earthquake" (Revelation 8:5). At the end of the seventh trumpet, "There were flashes of lightning, rumblings, peals of thunder, an earthquake, and heavy hail" (Revelation 11:19). At the end of the seventh bowl, "There came flashes of lightning, rumblings, peals of thunder, and a violent earthquake, such as had not occurred since people were upon the earth" (Revelation 16:18).

The "seven Spirits of God" take us back to Revelation 1:4, where the same phrase appears. Revelation speaks of "seven Spirits" as a way of referring to the fullness of the Holy Spirit. Seven is a number that represents completion, or perfection, in biblical literature; thus, this is speaking of the sevenfold Spirit.

New Testament scholar Gordon D. Fee comments, "[The seven Spirits of God] is rightly understood as 'the sevenfold Spirit,' imagery taken from Isaiah 11:2,[17] where it said the Messiah will experience 'the Spirit of the Lord' resting on him, who is then described with six Spirit-endowed qualities ('the Spirit of wisdom and understanding,' etc.)."[18]

The sea is another fascinating symbol in Revelation. To the ancient Jewish reader, the sea was a place of chaos and disorder. In contrast, heaven, being God's reality, has a sea, as well. This is not surprising, because Solomon's temple had a sea of bronze (1 Kings 7:23–26) and it was traditionally thought that Solomon's temple had hints of both Eden and of heaven. "Hebrews 8:5 calls the temple a 'copy and shadow of what is in heaven,'"[19] which advocates that Solomon's earthly temple resembles God's heavenly temple.

God's dwelling has a sea, but instead of raging and storming, it is calm and controlled. So tamed is the sea around God's throne that it appears as glass. Picture still water that reflects its surroundings. I think of the lakes in the Pacific Northwest that, when absent of people, are so still that they reflect the mountains and scenery around them. It is a serene experience to be near them.

Why is this "sea of glass" so important to us? Because God is not stressed about how history is unfolding; He is sovereign over it. He is not scrambling to find a game plan to counter the rebellious nations, for the political powers of this world do not get to tamper with God's plan.

The most chaotic natural force in our world, the sea, is at ease in God's reality. This should provide comfort to our anxious souls. We can have tranquility as we trust God, who is sovereign over all things. As the "sea" in God's sphere is contained, void of chaos, so God will one day make the same true "on earth as it is in heaven" (Matthew 6:11).

Richard Bauckham notes, "Heaven is the sphere of ultimate reality: what is true in heaven must become true on earth."[20] This is the final, future fulfillment of the Lord's Prayer found in Matthew 6:11. One day the reality of heaven will pervade the reality of earth and the chaos will be no more.[21]

The Song Without Cease

So worthy is the One on the throne that the four living creatures[22] "day and night...never cease to say, 'Holy, holy, holy, is the Lord God Almighty, who was and is and is to come!'" (Revelation 4:8 ESV).

This hymn of praise should not be seen as dry and monotonous, but as a celebration of God that never ceases to amaze us. His majestic holiness and beauty are worthy of a repetitive chorus.

I have heard some Christians complain when songs of worship have a chorus with repetitive lines. Well, they will truly be bothered by this song, then. Some songs are worthy of repetition because the object of the song is worthy of those words ten-thousand-fold and still more.

The holiness of God is the only attribute given such reference as to be emphasized with the threefold declaration. This is almost identical to Isaiah 6:3, where the Seraphim (literally, "the burning ones") were saying, "Holy, holy,

holy is Yahweh of hosts."

This rare threefold repetition draws remarkable attention to God's ontological uniqueness. His essence is utterly set apart, and there is nothing about Him that is tainted by sin. God's name, His reputation and character, are "holy and awesome" (Psalm 111:9c).

But sometimes we carry odd connotations into the discussion of holiness. We reserve the word for the "do-gooders" who are morally upright, and/or we limit the concept to being merely a synonym of, "moral."

While it certainly is not void of morality, holiness is richer in meaning. Holiness is ethical by implication, but ontological by nature. It is about *being* set apart more than *doing* set-apart things. The action is just the by-product of the identity. We are holy in that we are marked with purpose and affection. God is holy in that He is the purpose.

In Christ, who we are *is* holy. Touched by the divine grace, we become sacred people who belong to God's realm and are ambassadors of His realm.[23] And part of the Christian journey is growing in holiness as the triune God imparts His holiness into us (cf. Hebrews 12:8–14).

We may increase in God's likeness, but this is only to a certain extent. God's holiness is more than moral superiority; it is His utter uniqueness. He is holy, in that everything about Him is sacred, perfect, and worthy. Whatever glory He crafts us to have is only because He is the origin and source of such glory.

Heaven sings praises of God's holiness. And I can only imagine the quality of musical worship that is taking place there right now: the victorious celebratory songs, the songs that bring you to tears, and everything in between.

Oh, the splendor of the quality of musical worship that must take place in heaven! If our eternal destiny was *only* to sing the praises of our God (spoiler alert—it isn't), then it would be a glorious destiny.

Gordon Fee puts it eloquently: "All together this series of images is intended to inspire awe and wonder on the part of the reader, who is being brought into the presence of God, and before whom only awe and worship are the worthy responses."[24]

Casting Crowns

> And whenever the living creatures give glory and honor and thanks to the one who is seated on the throne, the one who lives forever and ever, the twenty-four elders fall down before the one who is seated on the throne and worship the one who lives forever and ever, and put down their crowns before the throne, saying,
>
> "You are worthy, our Lord and God, to receive glory and honor and power, because you have created all things, and because of your will they existed and were created."
> **—Revelation 4:9–11**

When I was a child, there were occasions when we would walk by a fountain and my mother would give my siblings and me a coin to toss in as we would make a wish. I was told of the fictional power of the fountain to hear our wish upon receiving a coin.

While the coin has inherent value, we considered paying homage to the fountain of greater value and of more appropriate use of the coin. The childish analogy is merely fun, but crowns are of no joking value, especially when God is the Giver of such crowns.

The twenty-four elders "put down," or, according to the translation I favor, "cast their crowns," before God (Revelation 4:10 ESV). We have already noted that these elders are representative of redeemed believers from both the Old and New Testament eras. They have received their crowns probably as a fulfillment of the promise of Revelation 2:10, where Jesus said that those who endure "until death" would inherit "the crown of life."

The word for "crowns" comes from the Greek word *stephanos*. It could suggest the victor's wreath given for winning an athletic event, or a crown that a person of royalty would wear. The imagery, I believe, is twofold, representing both.

The crowns are a symbol of the eschatological reward of eternal life for the overcomer (Revelation 2:10; 3:11; cf. James 1:12; 1 Peter 5:4). Those who wear these crowns will experience God's victory and blessing.

As a crown is a reward, it is merited by God's grace alone. Thus, it will be our privilege to do as the twenty-four elders do and cast the crown we receive before God, who alone is worthy of worship and honor and glory and power. This is our way of saying, "We only have this because You gave this to us; it is Yours, and we give it back to You in worship."

I hope to make silly moments like throwing coins into fountains into sacred ones as I tell my children, not about fictitious fountains, but about the infinite glory of God. One day we will cast our accomplishments before God and say, "You are holy, our Lord and God, to receive the glory and the honor and the power." Our victories, rewards, and crowns are not for our own glory, but for God's glory.

Anthony Hoekema anticipates this. "Some day," he says, "we shall cast all our crowns before him, 'lost in wonder, love, and praise.'"[25] This is a picture of something that believers do in heaven at the present; it is part of the worship and adoration of God in the intermediate state.

Equal Rewards

The reward of advancing the glory of God among the world is the fact that the glory of God is being advanced, and that we are permitted to play a role in such a worthy endeavor. I don't believe our good deeds will earn us any different rewards from other believers; this would miss the point.

The seven letters to the churches (Revelation 2–3) reveal that, despite there being a clear difference in degrees of obedience, all who end up enduring the faith will receive the same eschatological blessing.[26] What is true of the Church collectively is true of Christians individually.

Matthew 20:1–16 provides a parable of Jesus addressing this topic. I encourage you to read it and its surrounding context, but I will summarize its main point here. The parable is about a vineyard owner hiring various workers at different times of the day, but ultimately paying them all the same amount although some worked longer and harder than others. The famous, and incredibly misunderstood concluding line of the parable says, "The last will be first and the first last."

The point is that God's gracious reward is far beyond what we deserve to be paid, so we have no reason to complain that someone who becomes a Christian at ninety years old will receive the same reward as the Christian who has been faithful since age nine.

New Testament scholar Craig Blomberg comments on the passage: "[The parable] underlines God's ultimate perspective—all true disciples are equal in his eyes. That 'the last will be first, and the first will be last' ties the parable back in with 19:30. There the 'first' were believers; the 'last,' unbelievers. Here both 'first' and 'last' are believers. The terms do not imply unequal reward but reflect the order of payment. But if all are treated equally, then all numerical positions of ranking are interchangeable, and v. 30 applies at the spiritual level too.... There are no degrees of reward in heaven."[27]

If we have to be motivated by having a better eternity than our fellow brothers or sisters in Christ to do good works, then we miss the whole theology behind being made into a new creation. We have been given a new heart, and new affections, desires, and new virtues are formed.

We live the Christian life wildly abandoned to our previous life, not to earn our salvation or to earn some future rewards; we do so because we love God and we love people. The heart of Christ is being formed in us,[28] changing us from the inside out. Thus, the reward becomes the good work, and the good work, the reward. N.T. Wright agrees with my conclusion and adds some helpful insight of his own:

> It isn't a matter of calculation, of doing a difficult job in order to be paid a wage. It is much more like working at a friendship, or a marriage, in order to enjoy the other person's

company more fully. It is more like practising golf in order that we can go out on the course and hit the ball in the right direction. It is more like learning German or Greek so that we can read some of the great poets and philosophers who wrote in those languages. The "reward" is *organically connected to the activity*, not some kind of arbitrary pat on the back, otherwise unrelated to the work that has been done. And it is always far in abundance beyond any sense of direct or equivalent payment.[29]

What we do hear matters those
we remaine who we are
Now matters

Only God Is Worthy

Let us return to the text of Revelation 4. The crown-casting elders declare to God, "You are worthy, our Lord and God" (Revelation 4:11). The proclamation of God's excellency is not only true; it is countercultural.

In John's day, the triumphal procession of Caesar included the greeting, "You are worthy." It was common for Caesars to be considered deity, so the divine title of "Lord" was certainly used in political language, as well.

The book of Revelation is showing us here that only God is "worthy" and only He is the true "Lord and God." No political or royal figure can seize what belongs to God. After all, can anyone else claim to have "created all things"?

In the Greek text, there are definite articles attached to glory, honor, and power, which translates to "*the* glory and *the* honor and *the* power" (Revelation 4:11). This article is being utilized to classify and categorize the triad of praise. God doesn't receive *some* of the glory, He receives *the* glory—every ounce of it. There is no glory that categorically can compare to God's glory; His glory is the par excellence of all glory. And there is no one who gets to share in what is rightfully God's.

Our praise of God's greatness does not add any worthiness to Him; it is the rightful declaration of who He is before us and despite us. This is the type of worship we would expect to see in the psalter, like Psalm 96 for example, in which the psalmist declares the praises of God in His strength and glory and encourages the reader to ascribe Him similarly.

Sing to Yahweh a new song; sing to Yahweh, all the earth.

For all the gods of the peoples are idols, but Yahweh made the heavens. Splendor and majesty are before him; strength and beauty are in his sanctuary. Ascribe to Yahweh, you families of the peoples, ascribe to Yahweh glory and strength. Ascribe to Yahweh the glory due his name; bring an offering and come into his courts. Worship Yahweh in holy array; tremble before him, all the earth.
—Psalm 96:1, 5-9

The Hebrew word for "glory" is *kabod* which means "weighty." It is an understatement to say that God is the "heavyweight champion of the world." But God's glory is not some excess physical fat on His body; it is weighty in that it is full of substance.

Everything about His glory denotes majesty and meaning. The glory of God is, supremely, His presence. Where His presence is, there is blessing. Outside of God's presence is the antithesis of blessing. Therefore, we are designed to be glory-seekers, finding meaning in God and cherishing His glory.

God is the "one who lives forever and ever," making Him the Origin, Originator, and continual Sustainer of life.

In the doxology, He is credited as the Originator of life when the elders exclaim, "You created all things," a dominant biblical theme.[30]

This presupposes that God existed prior to what He created, and that nothing could have created God because God "created *all* things." In addition, God is the Sustainer of life. Hebrews 1:3 says that Jesus "sustains" and "upholds" all things in the universe "by the word of His power." So not only is Jesus the Agent of creation (John 1:3; Colossians 1:16; and Hebrews 1:2) with God (1 Corinthians 8:6), but He is also the Sustainer of creation (cf. Colossians 1:17). This is another way in which we recognize the deity of Christ through Him having the very essential attributes that belong to God alone.

Speaking of Jesus, where is He during this throne room scene? We see God the Father (the "One seated on the throne"), and we see the Holy Spirit (the "seven Spirits of God"). But where is the Messiah? Take heart! He is just moments away from entering the scene.

Excursus: Eternal Life

Christian jargon often extends the invitation to nonbelievers to "accept Christ" and to obtain "eternal life." Using the language of "eternal life" is not a bad thing; I only fear we fail to communicate the essence of what it actually is and leave it to the hearer to have enough biblical background to interpret the phrase accordingly.

This phrase is most common in John's writings. The concept takes two words into consideration—"eternal" and "life." While this phrase is not present in the book of

Revelation, it is certainly manifested through the apocalyptic imagery of "tree of life," "crown of life," "water of life," and "book of life."[31]

Eternal (Greek: *aiōnios*) life is *both* quantitative (pertaining to its duration; cf. John 6:51) *and* qualitative (pertaining to its condition or quality; cf. John 4:14). I like the way Elwell and Barry describe it in *Eternal Life*: "It is a mode of existence referred to in Scripture characterized by either timelessness or endlessness, and especially by a qualitative difference from mortal life."[32]

We do not merely obtain immortal life—there is a Greek word for that (*aphthartos*), which we do obtain (e.g., 1 Corinthians 15:52)—rather, we inherit eternal life. Immortal life is very specific, focusing on the unending nature of life without decay or death, while in the phrase *eternal life*, "the emphasis is on the quality of life rather than on the unending duration of life."[33]

However, immortal life is related, like a cousin, to the discussion at hand. According to 1 Timothy 6:16, God "alone," possesses immortality. Wright, accurately comments, "'immortality' is something which only God possesses by nature, and which he then shares, as a gift of grace rather than an innate possession, with his people."[34]

It is unfair to the biblical witness to infer the inherent immortality of mankind into the story, as this negates the symbolism of the tree of life and blinds us to the constant juxtaposition of God's way leading to "life" versus the antagonistic ways of rebellion leading to death or destruction.[35]

Proverbs 11:19, for example, tells us, "He who is steadfast in righteousness *is* to life as he who pursues evil *is* to death." Now the juxtaposition of life and death in Scripture is not limited to literal duration of life; while including duration, the juxtaposition also denotes metaphorical usage where the results of the two divergent paths are highlighted.

The word John uses for life is *zōḗ*, which is a transcendent, divine sort of life. This is to be contrasted with the Greek word for natural life, *bíos*.[36] John's theology of "life" is about the transcendent life that God possesses and shares,[37] first and foremost with His triune being, and secondarily with the beneficiaries of His grace. It is salvific in nature and implies the unending duration of eternal life plus the qualitative aspect.[38]

Zōḗ life can only be given by God, because He is the only One who inherently possesses it. When God created us in His image, He created us with the capacity to participate in His infinite love.

We are crafted with the intention to enjoy loving fellowship with the triune God, who in and of Himself has had loving community from eternity past shared by three equal but distinct persons. Richard Bauckham puts it this way: God, out of His grace, gives to His redeemed "new life which is so united to his own eternal life that it can share his own eternity."[39] This is eternal life—knowing God intimately (John 17:3) and participating in His eternality as a gift.

The biblical concept of eternal life is less like an unending line and more like a circle without beginning or end. By this illustration, we don't so much add infinite years to our life span as we become caught up in the eternality of God's life (analogously expressed as a circle), which transcends the measurements of time.

We don't invite Jesus into our lives. On the contrary, He invites us into His life, which He shares with God the Father and God the Spirit in intimate fellowship. The moment our faith in Christ unites our person to His person, eternal life becomes our possession as an inaugurated experience that will one day culminate in its highest potential.

This excursus concludes with the comforting words of Charles Spurgeon:

> *This life, being Christ's life, is an everlasting life.* "I give unto them eternal life," says Christ concerning his sheep. Somebody once said, "Ah, but they may lose it!" What nonsense! How can they lose eternal life? How can that be eternal which comes to an end? "Eternal life" must mean a life that never ends; language can only be meant to conceal men's thoughts if it does not mean that. But God uses language, not for the sake of concealing the truth, but in order to reveal it; and when the Lord Jesus Christ puts everlasting life into a believer, he has everlasting life, and he will live for ever, and for this reason, he will live forever because Christ will live for ever. "Because I live, ye shall live also."[40]

Eternal life is an invitation to participate in the life and love of God. God is not old; He is eternal. Eternal life is thus a present reality *and* a future hope.

WORKBOOK

Chapter Two Questions

Main Truth: God's throne is full of splendor and colorful light. There He is acknowledged and worshiped as He truly is—holy, holy, holy.

Question: What is the most beautiful, breathtaking experience you have ever had? What songs and Scriptures help you to anticipate the beauty and wonder of God and His throne room?

_____

_____

_____

_____

_____

_____

_____

_____

_____

_____

_____

_____

Question: What is the significance of the "sea of glass" in God's throne room? How can keeping a mental image of this throne room help you as you face stresses, difficulties, and sorrows here on earth?

_____

_____

_____

_____

_____

_____

_____

_____

_____

_____

_____

Question: In your own words, define _eternal life_ versus _immortal life_. Why is this distinction so important?

_____

_____

_____

_____

_____

_____

_____

_____

_____

_____

_____

Action: Read Matthew 20:1–16 and the surrounding context. What does this text teach about equal rewards versus degrees of reward?

Chapter Two Notes

_____

_____

_____

_____

_____

_____

_____

_____

_____

_____

_____

_____

_____

_____

_____

_____

_____

_____

_____

_____

CHAPTER THREE

The Scroll of Salvation

God has a definite plan for history and its consummation.
It is mapped out. It is set. It will not fail.[41]

—Daniel L. Akin

Read: Revelation 5:1–4

Revelation 5 is inextricably connected to Revelation 4.[42] Moreover, Revelation 5 helps us make sense of all the scenes of judgment that will unfold in the following chapters of the apocalypse. Revelation 4 and 5 go hand in hand. Chapter 4 is the setting, and chapter 5 is the drama. Chapter 4 highlights the throne of God and creation; chapter 5 highlights the Lamb of God and new creation.

We continue where we left off, entranced in a vision, viewing God's reality—heaven. At this point, everything seems like just another delightful day in heaven. Worship is going on, and God's world is unhindered by the chaos taking place on earth. However, we are about to see what moves the plot forward. Because God is very concerned about His creation, He is not satisfied until His definite plan comes to fruition.

Who Is Worthy?

And I saw in the right hand of the one who is seated on the throne a scroll, written inside and on the back, sealed up with seven seals. And I saw a powerful angel proclaiming with a loud voice, "Who is worthy to open the scroll and to break its seals?" And no one in heaven or on earth or under the earth was able to open the scroll or to look into it. And I began to weep loudly because no one was found worthy to open the scroll or to look into it.
—Revelation 5:1–4

A challenge is issued to the entire universe. A mighty angel's loud voice roars across the galaxy. Think about how powerful this angel's voice must be to call out to where no one "in heaven or upon the earth or under the earth" would be worthy to respond.

In essence, this is a scroll that demands only the one who is worthy to open it. John begins to weep "because no one was found worthy." We cannot miss this. What would cause John such anguish? What is the big deal about this scroll, anyway?

This is no ordinary scroll. Grant Osborne provides helpful insight: "The background is Ezekiel 2:9–10, where a scroll with words of 'lament, mourning, and woe' written on both sides of it is in the hand of God and shown to Ezekiel. There and here it is a message of judgment upon those who have opposed God."[43]

The scroll contains the righteous judgment of God and His plan to bring history, as we know it, to its appointed end, culminating in the birth of the "new heaven and new earth" (Revelation 21:1ff). It is the book of cosmic destiny for all of creation. It is the plan to take back and redeem God's world and rescue God's people from the adversaries of God.

John weeps, because if the scroll is not opened, then evil wins.[44] There is no greater feeling of hopelessness than what John weeps about here. This is how important the opening of the scroll is.

The scroll is held in the right hand of God, the hand of authority and power, thus requiring someone of equal stature to be able to take it from Him. It is sealed with seven seals, foreshadowing the seven judgments that would come from each seal being broken. Seven, again, is the number representing completeness, or perfection. So here we see a seal so perfectly keeping the scroll together that only someone worthy could break it.

Marvel's Thor comes to mind, as Thor's hammer can only be lifted by someone who is "worthy." But even Thor wouldn't be able to break the seals (primarily because he is a fictional character, but also because he isn't worthy like Jesus is). The whole universe was given the challenge, and no one could meet it. John's tears are completely appropriate. We all would be shedding tears if we were standing beside him in that moment.

Take note that the final goal of new creation requires a prerequisite action: the return of Christ to bring judgment and salvation. Judgment often has negative connotations, but the biblical concept can also be a celebratory thing because the reign of the Messiah means the reign of all that is good, bringing peace to the world. Contrary to some Christians' views, God doesn't separate the salvation of mankind from the salvation of the cosmos.

God's rescue is not about delivering us *away* from the physical creation, but *together with* the physical, ridding creation of sin's destructive presence. That is the purpose of this scroll, to bring God's salvation plan to fruition.

We have mentioned Psalm 96 already, but we have to revisit it, along with Psalm 97 and 98, because all three are relevant here. They personify various aspects of creation celebrating the coming judgment of God—because God's judgment is ultimately a good thing! (Seriously, read these Psalms.) His judgment brings deliverance from sin and evil and all that ruins humanity and creation. Believers should welcome the coming 'judgment' of God, in this sense.

If the scroll is not opened, then there is no justice that will be administered. And without justice administered, we have no salvation. And without salvation we have no new creation, which is the fundamental objective of the initial creation. The trajectory of mankind is so evil and perverse that it is only a matter of time until all is lost on man's own accord.

Without the opening of the scroll, we, and all the cosmos, are doomed. It is like an action flick in which time is ticking away, and evil is on the verge of victory—except this is no movie we are watching as a means of entertainment. John stands on behalf of all of humanity, watching our sobering hopelessness. And all that John currently sees is that no one is worthy to open the scroll of our salvation.

Heaven, we have a problem!

Behold the Lamb

> *And one of the elders said to me, "Do not weep! Behold, the*
> *lion of the tribe of Judah, the root of David, has conquered,*
> *so that he can open the scroll and its seven seals." And I saw*
> *in the midst of the throne and of the four living creatures*
> *and in the midst of the elders a Lamb standing as though*
> *slaughtered, having seven horns and seven eyes, which are*
> *the seven spirits of God sent into all the earth. And he came*
> *and took the scroll from the right hand of the one who was*
> *seated on the throne.*
>
> **—Revelation 5:5–7**

In some churches' children's ministries, it is not uncommon to find kids drawing pictures of certain biblical narratives. I have seen pictures of Noah's ark, Moses parting the Red Sea, and Jesus walking on water. However, I have never seen a child coloring a picture of Jesus in Revelation 5.

That is because not everything in apocalyptic literature is meant to be a congruent picture. You simply cannot draw a picture of the Savior who is described here. He is a lion-like lamb, standing but slaughtered, with horns, and the Holy Spirit all over Him.

The mixing of metaphors would be considered a big blunder by modern constraints, but for the ancient form of apocalyptic writing, it is completely acceptable. Each metaphor has imagery that communicates something about the subject, but if drawn out on paper would seem contradictory. We have to see what John is communicating about the

Lamb,[45] who is Jesus, as it informs us about the Christology of Revelation.

It is fitting that one of the elders, a redeemed believer himself, would be the one to console John in his weeping: "Behold, the Lion from the tribe of Judah, the root of David, has conquered." The victory has been won, as is communicated by the Greek aorist past tense.

The Lamb "has conquered," or "has prevailed." It is not an awaited event, but a past action that provides the foundation for the Christian's confidence. It has already happened!

Both titles—"the Lion from the tribe of Judah" and "the root of David"—are Messianic and originate in the Old Testament (cf. Genesis 49 and Isaiah 11); they see God as bringing peace on earth in and through the Messiah. The lion, an invariable symbol of strength and royalty, is applied to Jesus as the Messianic conqueror. The lion could also be representative of lion-like characteristics, as Proverbs 28:1b says, "The righteous are bold like a lion."

Later, in Revelation 22:16, Jesus calls Himself the "root and descendant of David." Coming from David's line, the Messiah was promised to take the throne of David and restore righteous rule. But this is a peculiar phrase; it is a paradox, indeed. How can He claim to be the root *and* the descendant of someone?

Remarkably, Jesus is the originator of David, as his Creator, and yet Christ also proceeds from David's lineage, as his descendant. This speaks to Jesus' hypostatic union, a theological term that encapsulates His true deity preceding from eternity past, and His true humanity, which joined His deity upon His incarnation. He is forevermore truly God and truly human—the "God-man."

John's mind must have been spinning with Old Testament Scriptures. His weeping ended abruptly. It is as if John's head, hanging low with his hands covering his tear-shedding eyes, had been lifted, and the removal of his hands restored his sight. In front of him, he saw not a roaring lion, but a slaughtered lamb.

Words cannot exaggerate his shock. It is not that John was unaware of Christ being the paschal lamb. But why would the elder tell John to look for a lion when he saw a lamb? The irony is found in the drastic contrast between a lion and a lamb. But the metaphorical description we are given about Jesus is that He is a lion-like lamb.

A Final Sacrifice

The language depicting Jesus as a "slaughtered" lamb is graphic, indeed. It comes from passages like Isaiah 53:7, which prophesied that the Messiah would be "like a lamb led to the slaughter." This makes us think of when John the Baptist cried out, "Behold the Lamb of God, the One who takes away the sin of the world" (John 1:29, my translation).

The paschal lamb would be the lamb slain at the annual Passover feast to atone for sin.[46] Jesus was crucified the day before Passover (John 19:14), becoming the first sacrifice of that Passover year and the final one for all who would trust Him.

Paul declares this glorious truth for believers: "Christ, our Passover lamb, has been sacrificed" (1 Corinthians 5:7b ESV). The annual feast finds its fulfillment in the slaughtering of the incarnate God. He appears before John as the slaughtered Lamb who stood in the place of sinners.

Both the words "standing" and "slaughtered" in Revelation 5:6 are set in the perfect tense in the Greek. This usage of the perfect tense communicates a completed action in the past that has continual results and ramifications in the present. Daniel L. Akin writes, "There is permanence about the scars of His sacrifice. There is also a once-and-for-all nature with abiding results to His sacrifice."[47]

And Leon Morris says, "The Greek perfect tense here signifies that the Lamb was not only slain at a point of time, but that the efficacy of his death is still present in all its power."[48] Christ's atoning death is so central to biblical doctrine that no tense other than the perfect could do justice to the language in this verse.

Christ will always be known as the slaughtered Lamb, and He will always have the wounds on His hands. It will be a token of His love for us and the sacrifice by which He rescued us. Charles Spurgeon says, "There is one mark in that hand which has made it specially dear to you, for 'the hand of the Lord' from which you receive everything is a nail-pierced hand, for it is the hand of the man Christ Jesus as well as the hand of the almighty God; and hard by the print of the nail is your own name, for he has said to you, 'I have graven thee upon the palms of my hands.'"[49]

Likewise, the Lamb's "standing" (also in the perfect tense) speaks of His resurrection and recalls Revelation 1:18, in which Jesus says, "I was dead, and behold I am alive forever and ever." Death could not contain the Lord of glory (Acts 2:24). We cannot ignore where He was standing: no place other than "in the midst of the throne."

He stands not where the rest of the layers of creation; He is at the center (cf. Revelation 7:17). That explains why the redeemed stand simultaneously in front of the throne and in front of the Lamb (Revelation 7:9). Christ is already standing beside the Father, who is on the throne. This makes sense in light of the later reference to the "throne of God and of the Lamb" (Revelation 22:3; cf. 22:1). While there is only one throne for God, there are two occupants. Likewise, God and the Lamb together form the temple of the New Jerusalem (Revelation 21:22).

We are told the Lamb has "seven horns," which are a symbol of perfect strength and kingly might. By using the number seven, the apocalyptic imagery leads us to trust that the Lamb is omnipotent, or, in other words, all-powerful. His "seven eyes" denote His omniscience—or His total knowledge. His omniscience is also demonstrated through the "seven Spirits of God who have been sent into all the earth."[50] This is a consistent way in Revelation to allude to the Holy Spirit. The Spirit being "sent out into all the earth" could be speaking of the Day of Pentecost "when the Spirit came upon the disciples and empowered them to take the gospel to the whole world" (Acts 1:8; 2:32–33).[51]

This appearance of what seem to be sporadic, mixed metaphors forms a consistent picture—not one that can be sketched out on paper—but one that can be grasped by the reader. This is the One who is worthy. He "took the scroll" (Revelation 5:7). He is heaven's answer to earth's dire need. A Champion has come to conqueror our catastrophic disease. He has rid our hearts of sin; now He will open the scroll and rid the world of the curse too. Whereas our damnation had a clock running against us, now our suffering is running on limited time.

Excursus: A Note on Suffering

Every worldview must provide a meaningful answer to the problem of suffering. Atheists will usually probe for answers among those who believe in the existence of God. Too often I have found Christians to be silent in giving answers to such vital questions. I hope that Christians would prepare themselves with compelling answers for this discussion so that skeptics can see the compatibility of Christianity with the reality of suffering.

I break it down to three key points:

1. **We see the world as it is, not as it should be.**

   The world we live in is post-Fall and pre-Eschaton. God's original creation was tarnished by the marring of sin. Because "sin" is that which goes against God's intention, sin is therefore the antithesis of God's design. God's design is good, but sin is what opposes God's goodness; therefore, it is not good.

   The Fall introduced suffering and decay of all sorts into the world. So, the world we see is post-Fall; it is not perfected by the governing goodness of God. The disorder of man's folly led to what we see now, and we know innately in our hearts that all is not as it should be. Our instincts are correct, and they should lead us to

God, who will set all things right by "making all things new" (Revelation 21:5). That is why we look forward to both the justice and the blessing of the Eschaton.

2. **God entered into our suffering to provide healing.**

Whatever our plight or our experience of suffering, God has known suffering more than we have. We do not have a God who looks upon our suffering without sympathy. On the contrary, our God knows our pain more than we could possibly give Him credit for.

God's desire to redeem us went to the extent of His becoming like us (the preexistent Lord became man in the incarnation, while maintaining His inherent deity). The One who never sinned, and who only did what was righteous, is the One who suffered the most out of all of the people ever existent in human history.

While we may not understand all the reasons behind our own suffering, we can trust God's infinite wisdom, in that all He has allowed to happen to us, He also predetermined the sacrifice of His Son to redeem us from it.

On the cross, Jesus took the heaviest dose of suffering, far beyond our comprehension. And now we have a great high priest who can understand our suffering, which helps to solve the emotional problem we might have, but not the actual dilemma. But keep reading, because…

3. **There is an unraveling plan meant to eradicate all suffering forever.**

God is not content with a world marked by suffering and evil, so He is unfolding a master plan to eradicate all suffering and evil— permanently. That is what the unleashing of the scroll is all about, which was initiated in Revelation chapter 5. So, although Christ is the paschal lamb who takes away our sins (John 1:29), He is also the roaring lion who will triumph over His enemies and secure true peace on earth forever!

Think of the time we have been given before the return of Christ as a time to repent. God's justice is delayed, not denied; the purpose of this delay is the grace needed for people who have not yet done so, to receive the mercy offered by faith in Jesus.

God Will Set All Things Right

In all honesty, everyone wants justice. When we were kids, we *wanted* our siblings to get caught doing something wrong. When someone cuts us off on the freeway and speeds past us, we *want* them to get a speeding ticket. And not only do we want that, but we want the satisfaction of watching the police car turn on their lights to pull them over.

But not all examples of justice are this immature or trivial. There are times when our desire for justice is, well, just. Think about the businessman who underpays his employees and hoards the money for himself. Think about the leader of a terrorist organization who sneaks away into the shadows uncaught. There are times when it is perfectly valid—and *right*—to seek justice. And these examples allow a just society to administer civil and sometimes militaristic justice.

However, when it comes to the biblical drama, the grand narrative in which we are living and taking part, it can feel like evil is reigning triumphant. It can feel as if God has grown calloused to all the suffering in the world caused by evil. But this is not the case. In fact, no one is more adamant about pursuing the end of evil than God. And He has a plan to eradicate all evil and reverse the curse that was set upon His creation.

When it comes to justice, make no mistake: God will administer it with great severity. God's enactment of His justice may be delayed for a time, but it is certainly *not* denied. We can rest assured that God will set all things right. And when He bangs the gavel of His righteous judgment, the entire world will feel the weight of it.

Until then, however, we should view God as acting mercifully toward people. The day of the Lord is coming, the day in which the wrath of God will fall upon unredeemed people. Every day that God's wrath is withheld is an opportunity for another sinner to come to repentance and find rest in the grace of Jesus Christ.

In this interim period, therefore, we are to be conduits of God's grace as we lead others to the same grace that we ourselves have experienced. It is our duty to give mercy even when it is not merited. We are to forgive the unforgivable that we see in others, because God has forgiven the unforgivable in us.

This is the part of history in which mercy is offered. This is our only chance to receive such divine forgiveness, as Hebrews 9:27 indicates that "it is destined for people to die once, and after this, judgment." And at the end of the day, we are not to be the ones who will take revenge, for "'Vengeance is mine,' says the Lord" (Romans 12:19).

WORKBOOK

Chapter Three Questions

Main Truth: The symbol of the scroll is the symbol of God's deed for cosmic salvation. Only Christ can open the scroll and save the world.

Question: What is the significance of the scroll in Revelation 5? What would be the consequences of leaving it unopened? What caused such a dramatic response from John?

_____

_____

_____

_____

_____

_____

_____

_____

_____

_____

_____

_____

Question: Describe the ways in which Jesus entered into our suffering while He was on earth. Does His identification with His people's suffering extend beyond the time He dwelt on earth physically? Why or why not?

_____

_____

_____

_____

_____

_____

_____

_____

_____

_____

_____

Question: What does it mean that "God will set all things right"? How does this understanding of the future inform and transform how we live presently?

_____

_____

_____

_____

_____

_____

_____

_____

_____

_____

_____

Action: List the major religions/belief systems of the world and each one's philosophy of suffering. How does Christianity differ from all others?

Chapter Three Notes

CHAPTER FOUR

The Coronation of Heaven's King

My desire is that my Lord would give me broader and deeper thoughts, to feed myself with wondering at His love.[52]

—**Samuel Rutherford**

Read: Revelation 5:9–10

We stand in awe and appreciation that the resurrected Christ ascended to heaven, the abode of God. This challenges our western concept of heaven as some immaterial realm. Because Jesus is both truly divine and truly human, resurrected from the dead, physical, yet not limited to physical constraints, we are forced to accept that heaven is far more material than we think.

This doesn't mean that its physicality is the same as ours; however, we must reconcile the idea that the different dimensions of heaven—God's dwelling, and earth, our abode—are closer than we think. And not only are they close in proximity, they are also close in rule. The One who rules heaven also rules earth. The Lord of heaven is also the Lord of the entire cosmos.

When thinking about the ascension, we also cannot help but wonder what happened to Jesus after He ascended into heaven at the end of the Gospels and the beginning of Acts.[53] How did the host of heaven receive Him? Was there a party that makes the grandest of ours here on earth seem pale in comparison? What happened? We shall answer these questions soon enough, but first we need to lay some groundwork.

The Royalty of Jesus

In Revelation 1:5, Jesus calls Himself the "firstborn from the dead." We see this title of Jesus being the "firstborn" also in Colossians 1:15, and "firstborn from the dead" in Colossians 1:18. Both of these verses are part of a passage that is highly significant to the discussion of Christology. The honorific title of "firstborn" is best understood in light of the immediate context of the passage where Jesus is referred to as the Son of God (Colossians 1:13–14), a title that Jesus is called regularly in John's Gospel; Jesus also refers to Himself as the "Son of God" in Revelation 2:18.

Jarl Fossum's *Son of God* points out that such titles as "firstborn" and "Son of God" carry a certain significance when applied to humans, which helps to uncover the even richer meaning when we are speaking of the unique divine Messiah.[54][55]

As the Son of God, Jesus functions as the mediator between those who are in union with Him (those who are "in

Christ") and the heavenly Father. His royal privilege was foreshadowed in the Old Testament, as kings, such as described in Psalm 89:27, would be exalted over all the other kings; Jesus is the Firstborn, the One who arrives as the substance of what was always a shadow prior to His royal arrival. Thus, Jesus serves as the eschatological, or the ultimate, fulfillment, and He functions as the true Son of God compared to all the failing shadows that had gone before.

When we speak of Jesus being the "Firstborn," we are referring to a position of privilege and preeminence. In Psalm 89:27,[56] the same Greek term for "firstborn" is used, but clearly not as a term for "being born first." Paul could have used a few different Greek words if he was trying to communicate that Jesus was created or formed before the rest of creation, but he didn't. Rather, it is a clear title of royal supremacy, in which God places the subject, the "firstborn," in the position of the royal ambassador of His divine presence.

Psalm 2 reaffirms this concept and establishes a predominant connection between the functional title "Son of God" and royal Messianic power.[57]

The language of 1:11 reflects Ps 2:7 and Isa 40:1. The point which appears to unite those two quotations is the kingly power associated with the title "Son of God" in the OT. While royal power is implied in the verse from Isaiah, where God's "chosen servant" (Isa 42:1) will establish "justice in the earth" (Isa 42:3b–4a), a task surely implying a king's power, the verse from Psalm 2 expresses the royal context outright. Originally an enthronement psalm, Psalm 2 was composed to celebrate the assumption of royal power by a king chosen by God to rule his chosen

> people and exercise vengeance over their foes who in opposing his people also opposed God. Verse 6 declares the enthronement; v 7 declares the enthroned king to be God's son, thus establishing the link between royal power and the title "Son of God" in the Psalm. That title is also used in the discussion of the establishment of a Davidic dynasty in 2 Sam 7:5–16. In that passage, Nathan announces God's will to David, and in describing David's eternal dynasty, cites God's promise that David's royal descendants will be "my son"—i.e., that "Son of God" will be a title for each succeeding king of Israel of the Davidic line.
>
> **—Paul J. Achtemeier**

Christ's life, death, and resurrection all serve in ways that contribute to Jesus being the Messiah who would bring God's royal rule to earth and redeem a specific people for God.

When Jesus ascended to heaven and was "seated at the right hand of God" (cf. Acts 7:55–56; Ephesians 1:20; Colossians 3:1; Hebrews 1:3), the idea came to fruition that God's universal reign has been inaugurated in and through the person and work of the Son of God, as noted in Peterson's commentary.[58] Colossians 1:15b reaffirms this, declaring that Jesus, as the "Firstborn," is preeminent over the scope "of all creation."

Our English word, "all" comes from the Greek word *pas*. This word is used in the singular, which helps bring a nuance to how every part of the whole is touched. In this case, the meaning is clear: There is not a single square inch of the universe that Jesus' preeminent Lordship does not cover. He is primary over every speck of creation. To summarize, calling Jesus the "firstborn of all creation" is best understood in the sense that Jesus is the prince who will inherit it all. It doesn't contradict His eternal deity, but also highlights a coming into kingly authority that was always destined to be His.

The Coronation

There is one more passage upon which we must comment before proceeding. Daniel 7 has perhaps the closest parallels to the book of Revelation, in genre at least. Daniel 7:1–8 begins the vision in which four beasts arise on the scene, representing various nations coming to power. In verses 9–12, the four beasts, or nations, are brought before the judgment seat of God (who is called the "Ancient of Days" in this passage). One beast is immediately destroyed, while the others are permitted to rule a little longer, but they are not outside God's sovereign ability to crush them, and He soon will. Then we come to verses 13 and 14.

The purpose of this passage is to show how the "Ancient of Days" will judge those who oppose Him and ultimately bring all people under subjection of the special figure who is like the "Ancient of Days" but also distinct from Him. Observe:

> I continued watching in the night visions, and suddenly one like a son of man was coming with the clouds of heaven. He approached the Ancient of Days and was escorted before him. He was given dominion, and glory, and a kingdom; so that those of every people, nation, and language should serve him. His dominion is an everlasting dominion that will not pass away, and his

kingdom is one that will not be destroyed.
                    —Daniel 7:13–14 *(CSB)*

Fyall's commentary on the book of Daniel clarifies that we are watching a coronation ceremony, in which the Ancient of Days crowns this strange figure who is "like a son of man."[59] This figure is about to inherit a kingdom that will be "everlasting" and "will not pass away." A strange ability of this figure is that he "was coming with the clouds"; in essence, he was riding the clouds. In the ancient world, it was believed that only a deity could ride the clouds.[60]

The description of this "son of man" closely parallels Christ's description of Himself (Matthew 24:30; 26:64; cf. Acts 1:11).[61] Even in the book of Revelation, Jesus is presented as the divine cloud rider (Revelation 1:7; 14:14–15).

If only there were enough time to unpack all the rich details of this passage. The important thing, as I mentioned, is this: Daniel 7:13–14 shows us a prophetic scene of the coronation of Christ foreshadowed in Old Testament apocalyptic imagery.[62] The Messianic cloud rider is being crowned as the King over all of creation, destined to rule with the Ancient of Days. The Messianic Lord, who now sits at the right hand of the Father, rules from heaven and oversees the events imprinted in the scroll of salvation.

Daniel 7 is the foreshadow of the ascension and coronation of the Messiah. Revelation 5 is the fulfillment of such an ancient hope. Christ has become King. Put more provocatively, God has become King.

Jesus the Prince

Part of the reason the Lord Jesus is revealed to us in this imagery as God's "Son" is because He is the Prince who rises to His royal reign within the chronology of redemptive history. Revelation 4 shows God the Father, who sits on the throne. I would suggest that Revelation 5 then presents a remarkable vision of the incarnate Son's ascension and coronation to the throne to be the "King of kings" (cf. Revelation 17:14; 19:16).

The events that take place are all part of the Son of God's coronation ceremony, after which He will rule heaven and earth alongside God the Father.[63] Trinitarian theology is inescapable in this passage as there is one God and one throne but multiple persons of God at the center of the throne.

The Gospels show us how the Lord, Yahweh Himself, inserted Himself into human history by becoming a man who then redeems and becomes King of His own creation. The narrative of the Bible really is the most phenomenal story; no man could have made it up, and we certainly cannot explore it enough. It is truly life-altering!

Crown him the Son of God, before the worlds began; and ye who tread where he has trod, crown him the Son of Man.[64]

—M. Bridges and G. Thring

A New Song

And when he took the scroll, the four living creatures and the twenty-four elders fell down before the Lamb, each one of whom had a harp and golden bowls full of incense, which are the prayers of the saints. And they were singing a new song, saying, "You are worthy to take the scroll and to open its seals, because you were slaughtered, and bought people for God by your blood from every tribe and language and people and nation, and made them a kingdom and priests to our God, and they will reign on the earth."

And I looked, and I heard the voice of many angels around the throne and of the living creatures and of the elders, and their number was ten thousand times ten thousand and thousands times thousands, saying with a loud voice, "Worthy is the Lamb who was slaughtered to receive power and riches and wisdom and strength and honor and glory and praise!"

—Revelation 5:8–12

The inauguration of the New Covenant naturally initiates the song of the chorus of heaven—a "new song." Again, Grant Osborne provides keen insight:

New songs are frequent in the Psalms, expressing a new worship inspired by the mercies of God (Pss 33:3; 40:3; 96:1; 98:1; 144:9; 149:1). In Isaiah 42:10 the new song is eschatological, looking ahead to the appearance of the Servant of Yahweh and "new things." There is a new kind of song to celebrate the coming of the new age that is soon to appear.[65]

Back in Revelation 4:8, we saw a song being sung to God by the four living creatures, and the text says that they "day and night never cease" to sing this song. Note that in Revelation 5:8–10, we see the four living creatures transition their worship in order to sing a "new song" to the Lamb.

What could possibly be a higher expression and identification of deity than to have the heavenly angels transition their unending song over to the worship of Jesus? What can stop the unceasing song of worship to God except something of equal value, namely the worship of the Lamb (who is also God—one with Him in essence, distinct in person). The moment the Lamb takes the scroll from God, Christ becomes the central object of worship in heaven, alongside God the Father.

The previous song was sung about God and the original creation; the "new song" is about the Lamb and the new creation. The definite victory of the Messiah calls for a new song, because now the dawn of the new creation has been inaugurated and the purchase has been paid for in full. This is even more spectacular than God's original creation of the world.

The One Who Is Worthy

Finally, in Revelation 5:9, we see the answer to the question posed by the mighty angel back in verse 2. "Who is worthy?" is answered by the worship and praise of the Lamb, who is declared to be worthy. This is not merely an ethical worthiness, although ethical worthiness is undoubtedly necessary.

Rather, this is an inherent worth, a sort of sufficiency to stand in equal authority with God to carry out the plan of redemptive salvation. The worthiness of the Lamb is credited not solely to His person, but more emphatically to His work—namely through His death and resurrection. Similar to the worship of the One on the throne in Revelation 4, the doxology of the Lamb focuses on His redemptive actions.

The chorus of heaven shouts the accolades of Christ's atoning sacrifice culminating in Jesus being our greater, and permanent, Passover Lamb.[66] The royal Son of God had a mission to accomplish, a conquest to champion, prior to being able to open the scroll. His ascribed worthiness is nothing short of the finished work of His Law-fulfilling life, His death-defeating death, His life-giving resurrection, and His throne-ascending ascension.

The original audience of the book of Revelation would have seen the natural comparison between the self-glorifying rule of Caesar and the self-sacrifice of the Lamb. The Lion of Judah secured the victory through sacrificing Himself as the paschal Lamb. Christ's way of conquering is countercultural no matter the era the reader comes from, whether the first century or the twenty-first one.

Allan Boesak observes that the Lamb "is worthy because his power is so completely different from that of the Caesar. It is a power not to destroy or to oppress but a power that is manifested in his love, in his willingness to give all of himself for the sake of those whom he loves. And in that willingness, in the power of that self-giving love, lies the liberation of his people."[67] Our adoration of Jesus' giving of Himself for the benefit of others motivates us to sacrifice ourselves for others at the drastic expense of our very own lives.[68]

The victory of God in and through the Messianic Lamb is decisive and done. This is the meaning of Jesus' wondrous words from the cross as He cried out, "It is finished"

(John 19:30). This powerful phrase is one Greek word, *te-telestai*. Remember the perfect tense of the Greek verb and its significance? Here is another example of how the original language of the Greek New Testament helps paint the dramatic effect of Jesus' sacrifice.[69]

In essence, it is said of Jesus: "All that is needed to pay for salvation has been paid in full; the transaction is complete." Not just any sacrifice would suffice, for our debt was infinite. Thus, the infinite had to become like the finite creation, and through the blood of God we have learned the weight of our sin and the love of our Savior.

The slaughtered Lamb forces us to contemplate both the holiness and the love of God. The Son of God who knew no sin also never knew a moment of separation from His Father until He tasted the separation we deserve. Because of what Jesus has done, we can cherish and anticipate the words that come from God: "Everything is accomplished" (Revelation 21:6a).

These words come following the judgment of God and the final judgment of all evil. The transaction has happened; the purchase was paid in full for our salvation. Now we await the full ramifications of the transaction, as God will judge the old creation and usher in the new creation, ultimately bringing substance to the words "Everything is accomplished."

We notice that the worship given to the Lamb in Revelation 5 is ascribed to His activity. When we celebrate the actions of God, we affirm the identity of God. For example, it is one thing to say, "God is good." This is, of course, true. But it is another thing entirely to say, "God is good *because...*" The key word here is *because*. The *because* gives reason to the reality.

His actions stem from His character. He is not inconsistent, like we human beings who oftentimes act against our very identity. The activity of God affirms what is already true of Him, what has always been true of Him. Because of that, we can worship Him with great confidence and delight.

The Multicultural People of God

The language of Revelation 5:9–10 demonstrates the twofold strategy of salvation to deliver believers *from* sin's penalty and power, and *for* royal identity and fulfilling service to God.[70] I agree with Leon Morris, who said, "Redemption is not aimless; [sinners] are bought so that they may belong to God (cf. 1 Corinthians 6:19–20)."[71] The verb here translated "bought," in Revelation 5:9, can also be translated as "purchased," or "redeemed." It is language of ransom as in a slave trade. The metaphor is that Christ has purchased the freedom of these people so that they would be free from their previous owner and come to be the possession of God. Being set free isn't about total autonomy; it is about belonging to a new owner. We are purchased by God and for God. But unlike anyone else, being God's possession is the source of infinite benefit and blessing. We are purchased by the blood of Christ, to be members of God's family.

The precious, powerful blood of Jesus is transformative, as it doesn't stop at performing a legal work (justifying us before God), but it continues to make something of us down to the core of our new identity. Thus, we become kingdom royalty, according to language that is familiar to the Old Testament covenant (e.g., Exodus 19).

Exodus 19:6, in the ancient Greek translation of the Old Testament (known as the Septuagint), says that God's people are "kingly priests." Mounce's commentary on Revelation shows that what was promised at Sinai, in the very context of Exodus 19, "is fulfilled in the establishment of the church through the death of Christ. Corporately believers are a kingdom, and individually, they are priests to God."[72]

"As a kingdom," Osborne writes, "they form the people of God, the new Israel experiencing a new exodus."[73] This is affirmed in Peter's letter, when he calls believers a "royal priesthood" (1 Peter 2:9), highlighting the reality of Christians being the Father's royal children.

The "kingdom and priests" motif encapsulates privilege and responsibility. Our belonging to God compels us to joyful service. Interestingly, God doesn't need anything from us. He is not as some of the Greek mythological gods were, who purportedly created humans to serve them.

In a drastic contrast, God created us with no necessity of our existence—but to glorify and cherish Him as He takes great delight in us as people created in His image. We were not made to serve the needs of God, but created with an invitation to join the life and love of the Trinity, reigning with God over His good creation. It has been the hope of human beings, ever since the earlier apocalypse found in Daniel, for the saints to receive "the kingdom forever, forever, and ever" (Daniel 7:18).

With that in mind, ponder this question: Is our duty as "kingly priests" something for us to step into now, or does that remain in the future? The answer is both. This is something eschatologically inaugurated, but with a greater and final fulfillment still yet to come. We will revisit the future aspect of our priesthood in Revelation 22:5.

As for our current situation, we are to be God's royal sons and daughters even now. God's covenant blessings, which we inherit even here on earth, come with the inheritance of God's mission. Our whole life and existence is inextricably tied to missiology. Thus, participating in the Great Commission (Matthew 28:16–20) is a responsibility because of our privileged relationship as followers of our Lord and His way. The Great Commission is about reaching the nations.

Psalm 82:8 provides a helpful backdrop to the expectation that God's people will be multiethnic. It reads, "Arise, O God, judge the earth, for You shall inherit all the nations." Because Christ has "purchased," or ransomed, us out "from every tribe and tongue and people and nation," we realize that God's intention has always been to create for Himself a multicultural people with which to maintain a covenant relationship.

The implications of this challenge the social barriers of any believer. Racism, unquestionably, has no place within Christianity in any way, shape, or form. Such arguments of ethnic superiority were dealt with by Paul (who himself was a Jew) in his letters to the churches in Galatia and the churches in Rome, for example. The distinction between Jew or Gentile (i.e., anyone who is not a Jew) is categorically irrelevant to the dignity and worth of a person who belongs to God.

Further ramifications include the notion that God celebrates the diversity of cultural nuance. This, of course, does not mean that He celebrates the worship of anyone except Him, or that He condones the ethics of anything contrary to His character, as revealed through His Word.

Instead, we are to look at the variations that distinguish us, culturally, with positivity, not with the attitude that one culture must eventually learn to conform to another. The sole "conformity" within Christianity is the conformity to Christ (Romans 8:29). We are united through biblical doctrine, but we are all unique in the cultural expression of our worship to the triune God. This is demonstrated through our native languages, styles of music, literature, and even festivities.

Humanity As God Intended

When a person makes an honest mistake, that person may say something to the effect of "I'm only human." This playful phrase reveals a lot about how we view humanity; part of this statement implies a correct assumption, but another aspect of it is absolutely wrong.

The correct assumption here is that we are all susceptible to errors of various degrees in our current condition. All too often, we choose what is averse to God's desired way of life, even against our good God-given conscience. But we must correct the wrong thinking in this idea as well. We cannot blame our "humanity" for being the way that we are. Being human is not the problem we must solve or from which we must evolve.

On the contrary, the answer is that we must become *more* human. Sin is the disease we have contracted, which is detracting from our true humanity, but God wants to restore it back to us. If being human was inherently the issue, then Jesus Christ rose from the grave as the wrong creature. In Christ, the Holy Spirit is transforming us from the inside out, moving us toward true human glory and reflecting the image of God as the crown of God's animate creation.

That is why those who trust in the Lord will find themselves becoming more human (as in bearing God's image), while those who reject the Lord will find themselves on a trajectory of becoming less and less "human"—until their humanity is lost altogether into oblivion. Thus, sin is not only offensive to God, it is offensive to our human potential. Although sin promises life, it ends in death—death to our humanity; instead of making us more human, it robs us of our authentic identity.

Ear-Shattering Worship

> And I heard every creature that is in heaven and on the earth and under the earth and in the sea and everything in them saying,
>
> "To the one who is seated on the throne and to the Lamb be praise and honor and glory and power forever and ever."
>
> And the four living creatures were saying, "Amen!" and the elders fell down and worshiped.
> **—Revelation 5:13–14**

What is the loudest cheering you have ever heard? How did you feel in that moment? What emotions were you experiencing as you celebrated among others without the slightest thought toward your dignity? If you are from

Chicago, maybe it was when the Chicago Cubs finally won the World Series. Or maybe it was during an encore song of your favorite band playing live.

Whatever the loudest cheering experience may have been for you, I guarantee you haven't heard anything like what we read about in the book of Revelation. Even Arrowhead Stadium, home of the Kansas City Chiefs, which set the record for the "loudest stadium" in 2014 at 142.2 decibels, cannot compare to this scene. To put this in perspective, if a helicopter were close by to you, its noise would be about 105 decibels, which is extremely uncomfortable to say the least. At 140 decibels, you are at extremely high risk to have permanent hearing damage.

Arrowhead Stadium needed over 76,613 cheering fans in attendance to break the record and reach a sound level louder than a jet airplane at 100 feet. Revelation 5:11–12 has already showed us an innumerable host of heaven glorifying and praising the Lamb. An immeasurable number! Imagine having so many people in attendance that you couldn't count them all! That is remarkable.

We arrive to the climax of worship in the throne room vision of chapters 4 through 5. The innumerable heavenly host shout their accolades of praise to the triune God in what I would imagine to be truly ear-shattering worship.

No wonder we will one day need glorified bodies, because such activities will require abilities we don't presently have. Our present ears could not endure such a cosmic worship set!

The worship proceeds. First, God the Father is worshiped in Revelation 4:8–11. Then Jesus the Lamb is worshiped in Revelation 5:8–12. Finally, God and Jesus are worshiped together in Revelation 5:13–14.

The inclusion of heaven, earth, the location under the earth (the underworld), the sea, and "all that is in them" stresses that nothing in all of existence is exempt from the great hymn sung to "the One sitting upon the throne and to the Lamb." It is difficult to imagine the ear-shattering volume of praise mentioned here. I can envision all of creation literally shaking as this took place. The adrenaline rush from this experience must be incomparable!

God and the Lamb

It is easy for us to recognize the worship that is due to God, but some skeptics—and many religions other than Christianity—fail to acknowledge the necessary worship of Jesus also. The deity of both God and the Lamb is central to Christianity.

Kostenberger poignantly says, "Jesus was not treated as an alternative object of worship alongside God. He was included in [the] worship of God."[74] God and the Lamb, according to Morris's commentary on the book of Revelation, "are joined in a way which is characteristic of this book (6:16; 7:9, 10, 17; 14:1, 4; 21:22, 23; 22:1, 3). There cannot be the slightest doubt that the Lamb is to be reckoned with God and as God."[75] Revelation 21:22 is the forthcoming eternal state, in which God and the Lamb are the "temple" of the new creation—they are the very centerpiece of all eternal worship.

We can learn a lot about worship from such chapters of the Bible. Notably, we are not told what keys to use or what aesthetics are preferred; rather, we learn of heaven's worship being completely theocentric—adoring and cherishing the triune God as the center of life and worship.

Revelation 5 appropriately ends in worship because it is indeed a coronation ceremony. Not only does Jesus take the scroll, which no one in all creation was worthy to do, but He takes His spot in the center of Heaven's throne with God the Father. There, God the Father and the Lord Jesus reign as King over all. The preexistent Lord who had appeared to Moses in the burning bush (Exodus 3), the Lord who was worshipped as Yahweh, humbled Himself to become a man. The Gospels record the journey of the Lord Jesus revealing Himself, redeeming mankind, and rising to His throne. The Son of God, the true Prince, is now at the center of the throne and the center of our worship.

The triune God is praised, sometimes as individual persons and sometimes as the unified God. Either way, the focus are the character, attributes, and redemptive actions of God. The more we point people directly to who He is, the more likely we will instiil confidence in the midst of our daily turmoil. We cannot understand the unfolding of redemptive-history outside a theocentric lens. God is the center and the goal of creation, and we must recognize Him as such before we are to make any sense of history itself.

The picture of God's throne room is a picture of absolute stability. We can possess total confidence in this life, because in God's reality, everything is sovereignly controlled. Despite the evening news showing constant tragedy, God *is* on the throne, He has a plan, and He is working all things for our good and His glory.

The Wrath of the Lamb

The wrath of God and of the Lamb is an unavoidable subject in the book of Revelation.[76] God's wrath is a necessary action, because God is love. It is only because the Lamb of God is loving that He acts in wrath, as the Lion of Judah, against anyone or anything that opposes the object of His love or the holiness of His character. We can observe a similar dynamic in human terms: Because I have a fierce love for my wife, anyone who would attempt her physical harm would experience my fierce wrath in my commitment to protect her.

I know people who claim they want nothing to do with God, but they still hope to "go to heaven" after they die. But why should someone who doesn't want to live for the glory of God now live eternally basking in the glory of God for eternity? Heaven is wherever God's manifest presence is, and where He is, He will be worshiped and glorified.

Heaven is only heaven because God is there. Heaven is a place dominated by God's prevailing presence! If someone wants nothing to do with God, then that person should want nothing to do with heaven, *because* not only is God *in* heaven—God *is* heaven! He is the very center of life in heaven, and He receives all the glory in heaven.

If those who oppose God are allowed into heaven, then heaven would become just another fallen world like this one. God gives us the choice to receive His grace or reject it; but with the natural ramifications that come with both. Reject God and you reject the Giver and Sustainer of life. Not only does God reject sin; but sin (by nature) rejects

God. In the end, rebellious mankind (unbelievers) get what it wants—autonomy from God. Ironically, that is called "hell."

As pertains to the duration of hell, there is a lengthy debate that has raged within orthodox Christianity. In my opinion, Scripture can be harmonized toward either position. For further study of the subject, I suggest *Four Views on Hell: Second Edition.*[77] Both positions on the duration of hell have nuances within the views and among those advocating the positions:

1. Eternal conscious separation from God, where the person will forever be in conscious misery outside of God's presence.

2. Annihilation—sometimes called "conditional immortality" or "terminal Punishment"—where the person will be destroyed permanently either instantaneously or after suffering for a specified amount of time.

Honestly, I lean towards the latter option. Annihilation seems to be the more biblical fate of the unbeliever. It also seems more consistent with the character of God, as I cannot imagine God taking delight in the eternal conscious suffering of people. However, the duration of hell is not an easy topic, and both positions have good validity and proponents for them. Both are united in the severity and finality of judgment for those who reject Jesus as Lord and Savior.

Old Testament theology develops a picture of a day

when God will come and judge the wicked of the world; this became known as the "Day of the Lord." Isaiah 63 is a chapter that tells of the Lord's coming judgment. Verse 4 reads, "For the day of vengeance was in my heart, and my year of redemption had come" (Isaiah 63:4 ESV).

Whoa! We clearly need a more awesome view of our Savior. I am not talking about "awesome" in the way we flippantly use the word today; no, I mean we need to be literally awestruck by the Son of God in His post-ascension glory and His passion for justice. I mean, essentially tattooed on His thigh is His identity as the "King of kings and Lord of lords" (Revelation 19:16).

No one can challenge Him, and no one can overthrow Him and His kingdom. He has ascended to the throne and no one will dethrone Him. Not even the devil himself has the power to do so (not even close!). Jesus' humble humanity has become glorified; His coronation has granted Him the ability to show forth His true nobility. The Lord of glory has taken His place on the throne.

He now appears as you would expect the King of the cosmos to appear—radiating light, as the light and beauty of creation only reflects the majesty of its Creator, powerful in stature, as is symbolized by His seven horns and His riding a white horse in Revelation 19.[78]

So, we are told in both Isaiah 63 and all throughout the book of Revelation that our Savior is very concerned about justice being served. But unlike us, God's justice is always redemptive in its purpose. I appreciate the helpful note from Old Testament scholar John Oswalt on Isaiah 63:4:

The reader may reply, what about that word vengeance?

Does that not convey a mean spirit of revenge and bitter-
ness? It might if it were by itself, but the parallelism here
shows that is not the case. What is the vengeance about?
God's hurt pride? No, it is about redemption, about break-
ing the power of sin and evil so that those who are held in
its grasp may go free. This is precisely the point that the
Servant/Messiah made in 61:2 in similar words (and one
more reason to recognize that all of the work of that person, both salvific and judgmental, is included here). God's
purpose in destroying evil is never merely an end in itself.
It is always in aid of a larger one, the deliverance of the
faithful.[79]

The book of Revelation says that Jesus' eyes are "like a
blazing fire" (Revelation 1:14; 2:18; cf. Daniel 10:6), a
symbol of His fierce opposition to His enemies. The King
on the white horse has fire in His eyes, because He is zeal-
ous to secure safety for His people. The divine warrior has
the "day of vengeance" in His "heart" because He has the
salvation of His bride in His eyes.

All this describes the Lamb of God, Jesus Christ, who is
also a lion-like King coming to establish His kingdom on
earth and destroy any who willfully oppose His rule. This
is our Lord, before whom we should tremble in awe, yet
whom we should worship in adoration.

Paving the Way for the New Creation

Imagine you're reading a book to someone, perhaps
your child or a friend. As you read a book aloud to others,
it is not that the words are being written as you read them;
to think so would be absurd. The words were written on
the pages prior to the reader experiencing them in their se-

quential order. And so it is with human history.

As much as humanity likes to think that the ultimate direction of human history is still up for grabs, that is a façade and a lie. The end goal of human history is already written and contained within the scroll—written by God and carried out by God.

We are only seeing, and will continue to see, the unfolding of the story that was written before the foundation of the world. The Lamb of God is the only One worthy to carry forth, as a commander, the orders contained within the scroll.

The majesty of the triune God ought to eclipse any worries that plague our days. Revelation 4–5 provide us with a theocentric (vertical) vision, which allows us to see the vanity in any anxiety provoked by what is in front of us (horizontally).

Charles Wesley writes:

> Still the atoning blood is near, that quench'd the wrath of hostile Heaven: I feel the life His wounds impart; I feel my Saviour in my heart.[80]

Do you experience what Charles Wesley did? Do you "feel the life His wounds impart"? The Lion-Lamb has been slaughtered so that we can be ransomed. His blood has set us free and pays the price so that we can be made new. The *full* blessing of God is still yet to come, but it is already inaugurated upon us.

The Lamb is unfolding the sovereign plan to take back the earth from the depravity of sinful people, to eradicate the evil, and to move the earth beyond its original creation and into its fullest intention. Ultimate victory has already been secured by the finished work of the Messiah. God's salvation for His people does not rescue them away from the world, but rescues them to the world and for the world, anticipating the glorious renewal of the world and all the cosmos at the end of human history.

What we see carried out in the rest of Revelation is simply the administering of the ramifications of Christ's victory—triumphing over His enemies and ushering in the dawn of the new creation. I wish we had time to elaborate on chapters 6 through 20 of Revelation, but to stay concise and focused on the theme of new creation, we must push forward. What you need to know about Revelation 6-20 is how that portion of Revelation paints the picture of God's judgment in coming against the cosmic and earthly; the spiritual and human rulers. In His life, death, resurrection, and ascension—Jesus now has accomplished a definitive victory, with impending implications still to come.

The eloquent words of Grant Osborne paint this picture: "Christ has become the Lion, the royal Messiah, by becoming the slain Lamb. His death on the cross is the true central event of human history, and through his sacrifice the paschal lamb has become the conquering ram who will end this world of evil and usher in eternity."[81]

As the Prince of Heaven has ascended to the throne, has He ascended to the throne of your heart and your affections? As the victorious Christ stands at the center of the throne and takes the scroll, He displays how worthy He is, and He is worshipped in light of His triumph. How could anyone or anything be worthy enough to stand at the center of our focus? As He prepares to finish the task of justice, promising to return to the world and free it from all evil, sin, and the curse, His eyes blaze with fire—He shines with glory. How can anyone eclipse His majesty? Worship the King of kings and Lord of lords! Join the chorus of angels and saints in celebrating the coronation of Heaven's King!

The Climax of the New Creation Is Coming

Read Revelation 6–20

> Be heaven even now our soul's abode, hid be our life with Christ in God, our spirit, Lord, be one with Thine: let all our works in Thee be wrought, and fill'd with Thee be all our thought, till in us Thy full likeness shine.[82]

Every narrative, whether it be book or movie, has a climax. All preceding moments build up to the climactic moment. Maybe it is the man expressing his love for the woman he has been chasing throughout the whole movie, or perhaps the hero finally triumphs over the villain. Whatever it may be, every story has a climax. Get ready to feel the elation of emotion as the climax of the book of Revelation unfolds starting in Revelation 21. Behold! Everything is new!

WORKBOOK

Chapter Four Questions

Main Truth: At His ascension, Christ was crowned King of creation. He now rules with God on the throne as the plan of God unfolds to bring forth the consummation of the new creation.

Question: What does the ascension of Jesus in a material, human body tell us about the nature of heaven?

_____

_____

_____

_____

_____

_____

_____

_____

_____

_____

_____

Question: Why does the ceaseless song of heaven change in Revelation 5? What is the significance of this new song?

_____

_____

_____

_____

_____

_____

_____

_____

_____

_____

Question: How are the people of God described? What is the meaning of each of these titles?

_____

_____

_____

_____

_____

_____

_____

_____

_____

_____

_____

_____

Action: Plan and prepare for a meaningful worship experience. This could take place in a church setting, at a Christian event, while observing natural wonders, or with a group of close friends. During this time of worship, reread Revelation 5. Try to make the worship as Christocentric as possible. Meaning, try to choose songs or write lyrics that focus solely on who Jesus is and what He has done.

Filioque Clause —

Chapter Four Notes

Jesus: not a part of creation – always
been – is God

God's
OT – Judgment – Redemption

The shack

Book: When God Became King
N.T. Wright

The Wedding of Two Worlds

There will never again be an earth "down here" and a heaven "up there."[83]

—**Grant R. Osborne**

Read: Revelation 21:1–4

Attending a memorial service for a fellow brother or sister in Christ is a complex emotional experience. In one sense, we are happy for their security in the Lord and the comfort that comes from this Christian hope. In another sense, we are saddened not to be able to see them on this side of life anymore. Either way, tears are an appropriate response—whether they be tears of joy or tears of sorrow.

Listening to believers speak of the deceased provides a fascinating exposition of contemporary eschatological theology. While I appreciate the sentiment of what is usually spoken, rarely is someone elucidating an accurate, biblical view of the afterlife of the believer. I don't think less of the individual, unless it is a pastor—who should know better. Let's pretend it is a man named John's funeral. Here are a few examples of what is typically said: "I know John is singing with the angels in the clouds and that we will one day join him in singing to God for all eternity." "John is dancing on streets of gold right now!" "John is probably looking down on us, watching out for all of us."

Here is the thing. The sentiment of those statements is kind and meaningful, but they are not correct. "Heaven" does not consist of an everlasting worship set, continually singing the crescendo of our favorite worship hymn for eons and eons. "John" is not on streets of gold on the new earth—no one is, yet. And lastly, "John" is probably not concerned with his own funeral when he gets to be in the presence of God.

For souls in the intermediate state ("heaven," as it is currently prior to the eschaton), there is more that is chronologically yet to happen. The intermediate state is not a static state. It is not our final destination. There is still a sense of waiting and expectancy, even for all believers who are there. Heaven is a transient place; a dwelling with an incomplete journey. Heaven is a world waiting for its wedding.

Jesus' words in John 14:2, "In my Father's house are many dwellings," are typically quoted as referring to the eternal state, but it is actually about the intermediate state. The word for "dwelling places" here, *monai*, is regularly used in ancient Greek, not for a final resting place, but for a temporary halt on a journey that will take you somewhere else in the long run.[84]

Our fellow brothers and sisters in Christ who have gone on before us *are* present with the Lord, genuinely in bliss, but they are also awaiting the resurrection of the body and the ushering in of the universe made new. Anthony Hoekema says of the saints in the current heaven, "...their happiness will be provisional and incomplete. For the completion of their happiness they await the resurrection of the body and the new earth which God will create as the culmination of his redemptive work. To that new earth we now turn our attention."[85]

And so now we, too, turn our attention to the consummation of the new creation. As we enter what Revelation has to say about the eternal state, we cannot look for answers to questions that are not asserted by John's vision. The book of Revelation addresses eschatological questions that an ancient Jew would ask, not a modern American—questions like, "Will death exist? Will chaos continue? What will be the fate of the temple?"

Not everything we want to know about the eternal state is made known. Some parts we get to see, and so let's cherish every detail of those. There will be things we can make good biblical conjectures about. And then there will be things we would like to know about, where the Bible is simply silent, and so we must be, as well.

As for how the ancient letter wishes to encourage us, the layout is as follows:

- God's cosmic new creation (Revelation 21:1–8)

- God's global temple (Revelation 21:9–27)

- God's escalated Eden (Revelation 22:1–5)

A Kainos World

Genesis 1:1 says, "In the beginning God created the heavens and the earth" (ESV). If you flash forward from there to the prophet Isaiah, you will notice that he speaks of the radically new and redeemed creation, and his words bear a remarkable resemblance to the wording of Genesis 1:1. This is found in Isaiah 65:17a: "For behold, I create new heavens and a new earth" (ESV).[86]

Now we come to Revelation 21:1: "Then I saw a new heaven and a new earth. For the first heaven and the first earth passed away and the sea no longer exists." The word "new" here seems to be jumping off the page at me as I read the text. It is hard to ignore such a refreshing word!

The Greek word for "new" in this passage is *kainos*, the same word used in the Greek Septuagint in Isaiah 65:17 (mentioned above). This is a fascinating choice of word in that it denotes a "qualitative distinction," as stated in G.K. Beale's commentary.[87]

The new heaven and the new earth are "new" in that they far exceed and eclipse the previous creation. Behm's definition of *kainos* reveals that the word emphasizes "what is new in nature, different from the usual, impressive, better than the old, superior in value or attraction."[88]

Within the newness, there is both a continuity and a discontinuity of the new creation. There is also a totality in scope of the new creation. Just as Genesis 1:1 sums up the creation of all things, Isaiah 65:17 and Revelation 21:1 (cf. also Isaiah 66:22; 2 Peter 3:13) describe the extension of the *kainos* creation to expand out to the entire creation.

Behm explains, "New creation is the glorious end of the revelation of God's salvation. It is the supreme goal of early Christian hope."[89]

The newness by which the new creation will be marked is freshness. It is the superlative, the highest good, exceptional in quality and condition. In his commentary on Isaiah, Motyer says, "Everything the Lord created at the beginning will be made new at the end."[90]

The heaven that will be made "new" is not the heaven of God's presence, but the layers of atmosphere and the starry expanse that encompasses the universe. "Heaven and earth" is a biblical merism, a designation constituting the entirety of the cosmos.[91]

There will be no differentiation between the heaven of God's realm and the heaven of our realm. And the earth that will be made new isn't some far-out, different earth. It is *our* earth that will be made glorified in newness, just as we ourselves will be glorified in newness. Everything won't only be created new, everything will always remain new—enduring in an irreversible freshness and vitality.

A Sea-less Existence

And I saw a new heaven and a new earth, for the first heaven and the first earth had passed away, and the sea did not exist any longer.
—Revelation 21:1

Many people I have spoken to have lamented at the second part of Revelation 21:1. They read about the absence of the sea, and they are saddened that there won't be beautiful, recreational oceans in the new world.

Once when teaching a class on biblical interpretation, I used this passage as a means of helping students better understand the importance of reading the Bible not *literally*, but by its *literary genre*.

For example, you would not read the book of Proverbs the same way you would read the Gospel of Mark. Why? Simply because among the many differences is the distinctive difference in genre and the ways in which the author uses different literary styles to convey his message.

The book of Revelation is either too feared or not revered enough by many. What I mean is that some Bible-believing Christians stay away from it their whole lives, too afraid to take the time to understand it, and thus miss out on the blessed message of the book. Yet others consider the language plainly and read Revelation with no consideration to the genres at work, leading to many egregious misinterpretations of the book.

Revelation is an epistle, a book of prophecy, and apocalyptic literature. Contained within it are hundreds of Old Testament allusions and imagery, and the constant usage of symbols gives shape and color to its message.

The absence of the sea as described in this book is a prime example of symbolism at play within the book of Revelation. Why would John speak of the comprehensive scope of redemption (in heaven and in earth, in the cosmos and in our world) but then randomly throw in a geographical detail about the new world?

John is not saying, "There will be no oceans in the new creation." Before you put down this book and walk away, though, hear me out. We must insert ourselves into the world of the author and the choice of genre he is using to communicate.

Back in Genesis, we saw a "good" creation, but not a consummated creation.[92] The sea is described as chaotic and wild. Then consider how God pronounced judgment upon the world in Genesis 7—with a worldwide flood. God even used "the sea" as a means of crushing Pharaoh's armies in the book of Exodus.

Now turn to Mark 4:35–41 and observe how fearful the disciples were as a storm raged upon the Sea of Galilee, threatening their lives. Let's camp there for a moment. There have been gigantic ships, cruise ships and otherwise, that have sunk to the depths either because of storms or due to other elements in the sea.

If even our modern technology cannot fully prevent the turmoil of the sea, then imagine how the disciples' fishing boat stood any chance in comparison! (Spoiler alert—they would have died if it hadn't been for Jesus' presence on the boat.) The Jew was no sailor, and the sea was a feared place where many corpses had been buried.

This doesn't even include all of the biblical examples of where the sea, while being a literal entity, also provides keen insight into what it might symbolize. But then we arrive at Revelation, where the sea is seen prior to its arrival in chapter 21. The "sea" (Greek: *thalassa*) is used twenty-three times in Revelation alone. Those uses show the sea as being the presence of the beast (Revelation 13:1), into which Babylon the Great will be (metaphorically) thrown as a place of banishment (Revelation 18:21) and as a graveyard for the dead (Revelation 20:13).

We also must not forget that John had been banished to the island of Patmos and was separated from the beloved churches to whom he wrote. He could walk onto the shore and look across the sea, staring at the vast expanse that had separated him from his church family. In summary, we can gather from the biblical data that the sea is a primary symbol of chaos, the origin of cosmic evil, the place of the dead, and a large chasm separating people from one another.

But there is a peculiar appearance of the sea in Revelation 4:6. As we have already seen, this chapter of Revelation pulls back the curtain and shows God's reality as He rules from His throne. We encounter some astonishingly curious imagery, but then we are told that before the throne of God, there was a "sea like glass, like crystal."

Have you ever gazed upon a lake with water so still that it appeared as glass? It is quite a sight. Sometimes you can even see nearby mountains reflected in the water. It is a peaceful place, serene indeed. Whether God literally has a "sea like glass, like crystal" at His throne or not is irrelevant. The information is in the imagery. Despite the absolute disorder being visited upon the world due to fallen humanity's acting contrary to God's design, God's reality in heaven has order and is totally tamed.

There is nothing in heaven that is threatening the peace of God's rule or those in His presence. In His incarnate ministry, Jesus proved to be the true embodiment of heaven on earth as He restored dead or decaying things to life (in His healing ministry) and brought peace to the chaotic forces of this world (in calming the sea). He foreshadowed His divine ability to bring harmony back to the hazardous creation, as the Bible promises will happen.

Revelation 21–22:5 is unique, in that it is presenting

something exclusively in the future, the awaited consummated creation, which is also known as the *eschaton*. At the eschaton, God's reality, as it is in heaven, invades and pervades everything. Not a single square inch is untouched by His redemptive power that is "making all things new" (Revelation 21:5).

The sea being removed indicates the removal of the chaos of the previous world and the removal of the grand graveyard that will no longer be needed—for all who live on the new earth will never go to the grave. Death will become a distant memory and an eradicated reality.

Anthony Hoekema says in his book *The Bible and the Future*, "Since the sea in the rest of the Bible, particularly in the book of Revelation (cf. 13:1; 17:15), often stands for that which threatens the harmony of the universe, the absence of the sea from the new earth means the absence of whatever would interfere with that harmony."[93]

Charles Spurgeon once wrote, "Scarcely could we rejoice at the thought of losing the glorious old ocean: the new heavens and the new earth are none the fairer to our imagination, if, indeed, literally there is to be no great and wide sea, with its gleaming waves and shelly shores."[94]

I truly believe that the new earth will contain majestic beautiful oceans, lakes, and rivers.[95] The absence of the sea in Revelation is the absence of anything that would threaten life and God's rule. So, watery expanses will still prevail, but without the threat of hurricanes, or a fatal shark attack, or any other threat. While chaos has marked human history due to the Fall and mankind's constant rebellion against God, the new creation will be marked by harmony and goodness.

I am convinced that our oceans and beaches will still be there to proclaim the glory of God, but they will be unhindered by the marring of sin, and they will be a place of many recreational activities, both familiar and unfamiliar to us now. I can only imagine what the new Hawaii will look like! Remember, everything will be new; it will all be *kainos*. It will be superior to the first creation. I can only imagine what beauties and activities will await us as we dive in to the delight of the new oceans.

On our honeymoon, my wife and I had the privilege to go to Jamaica. The months of saving up paid great dividends as my wife, Ariana, and I enjoyed the warm sun, the delicious food, and the starry nights. Undoubtedly, my favorite activity was snorkeling. You must realize that my biggest fear is being attacked by a shark, so this was kind of a big deal for me.

As we plunged into the water, we swam among fish of all kinds and colors. Reefs had plants that danced and swayed with the rhythm of the ocean. I swear I had a smile on my face through the mask the whole time. We took our GoPro with us to video-record the experience, and each time I came back to the top of the water, I exulted God in worship!

Every second, in every movement, I experienced God's presence and His goodness. No one can convince me otherwise; I was communing with God, enjoying His company and celebrating the work of His hands. It was new, fresh, and refreshing. Life was vibrant, and I was basking in the creations of my Creator. That day, maybe more than any others previous, I learned that recreational activity in God's creation can promote some of the most fervent and heartfelt worship to God.

I have had a few individuals challenge me on this, say-ing something along the lines of: "We will be worshiping God for all eternity! How does your idea of snorkeling fit into all of that?" It is a valid question. I *do* agree that we will be worshiping God in all we do for all eternity. And I believe that includes recreational activities. If you have not learned how to do any activity to the glory of God, then you have yet to experience life with your total person en-gulfed in God's presence and His creation in perfect harmony.

My point is this: Worship is not only a song we sing; it is a life we live. Everything that is not inherently sinful has the potential to be glorifying to God and enjoyable to us.[96]

Heaven on Earth

And I saw a new heaven and a new earth, for the first heav-en and the first earth had passed away, and the sea did not exist any longer. And I saw the holy city, new Jerusalem, coming down out of heaven from God, prepared like a bride adorned for her husband. And I heard a loud voice from the throne saying, "Behold, the dwelling of God is with humani-ty, and he will take up residence with them, and they will be his people and God himself will be with them.
—Revelation 21:1–3

It is self-evident that life is not the way it should be. If you have ever watched the show *Planet Earth* (which is an exceptional show, except for its unfortunate evolutionist worldview), you will quickly discover how the circle of life involves a constant struggle for survival.

Admittedly, my favorite part of the show is the phenomenal scenery. It shows some of the most gorgeous landscapes nature has to offer, along with the creatures that live in the various terrains. However, the show does not shy away from the fact that nature is both hostile and decaying.

Some people think they desire to live in a tree house in the tropical jungles of Brazil, but we are not naïve; there are a thousand ways we could die from positioning ourselves in such a dwelling.

Even more common recreational activities, like camping in the United States, are not void of danger. Whether it be the risk from animals, such as grizzly bears, or from poisonous plants, or from other inherent dangers, there are many ways in which it can seem like nature is trying to kill us off. Perhaps we can find solace in the fact that the Bible addresses this.

A person with an atheistic worldview and I were dialoguing. I was telling him of the special love God has for humanity. One moment his arrogance shone through as he asserted his question: "We have discovered that there are millions of planets throughout the universe. What makes you think Planet Earth is so special?"

I smiled and replied, "Because no other planet is meant to become the home of God." This, of course, required much further explanation, in which we began talking about the cosmological differences between his perspective and my biblical worldview. It was a good conversation.

I bring this up, because many Christians would scoff at my answer to his question. They might say something like, "Surely God won't live on earth! He lives in heaven!" But that is precisely my point. Heaven is "heaven" because God is there. But earth will become heaven, too, because God will make His dwelling *here*. That is the wonderful truth behind Revelation 21:3. The home of God and the home of man will be one and the same.

Anthony Hoekema writes, "The 'new Jerusalem'…does not remain in a 'heaven' far off in space, but it comes down to the renewed earth; there the redeemed will spend eternity in resurrection bodies. So, heaven and earth, now separated, will then be merged: the new earth will also be heaven, since God will dwell there with his people. Glorified believers, in other words, will continue to be in heaven while they are inhabiting the new earth."[97]

Biblically speaking, "heaven" is the abode of God; it is where God dwells.[98] So, when the passage says that the "dwelling of God" will be with mankind, it is saying that heaven itself will be with mankind. The life of heaven and the life of God are the same thing. Matthew's Gospel goes as far as using the phrases "Kingdom of God" and "Kingdom of heaven" as synonyms.

When we proof-text the phrase "blessed are the meek for they shall inherit the earth" (Matthew 5:5), we have to remember that just two verses earlier, the "poor in spirit" are "blessed" because "theirs is the kingdom of heaven." It is not that the poor in spirit and the meek inherit different places; that would be absurd.

The poor in spirit are also the meek, simply described in different verbiage; thus, all the "rewards," per se, in the Beatitudes are different pieces of the same puzzle. To inherit the "kingdom of heaven" is the same as inheriting the earth, in the sense that the destiny of the kingdom of heaven is to come down and marry the earth.

For the first time ever, God will finally, fully, and forever make His home on earth, where all of creation will feel His presence like never before. The two worlds, for the first time, will be wed. The realm of God and the realm of man will intersect, becoming inseparable and indistinguishable.

God's love, goodness, power, and beauty will touch every part of His marred creation, making it all *kainos* new. There won't be a single speck of the universe that isn't "heaven," since the entirety of creation will be captivated by the presence of the triune God.

I like the way Hoekema puts it: "From verse 3 we learn that the dwelling place of God will no longer be away from the earth but on the earth. Since where God dwells, there heaven is, we conclude that in the life to come, heaven and earth will no longer be separated, as they are now, but will be merged. Believers will therefore continue to be in heaven as they continue to live on the new earth."[99]

Heaven and earth will be indistinguishable and inseparable, because they will become one. Heaven will be earth, and earth will be heaven. Grant Osborne is right on when he states: "There will never again be an earth 'down here' and a heaven 'up there.'"[100]

Of course, this doesn't mean that heaven is literally above us while the earth rests below it. The ancient language of heaven being "above" is metaphorical, describing the higher form of life associated with heaven. It is like when someone receives a promotion at work; it doesn't mean that they necessarily move to an office on the floor literally above. That would be missing the point.

Romans 8, which speaks about the Christian's release from condemnation, includes some verses that speak of creation's eventual release from the curse of sin. Verses 21 and 22 demonstrate that all of the physical creation awaits the blessed effects of redemption.

God's "making all things new" (Revelation 21:5) applies not only to people, but also to creation. In Romans 6:18, 22, and 8:2 the same verb for "set free" is used, applying to human freedom from sin's penalty and power. Now Romans 8:21–22 reminds us that even the physical nature needs more than a makeover; it needs to be *made new*. That is why even the most beautiful sunset you see is still a broken sunset, marred by sin, still in bondage to the curse upon all creation, awaiting the effects of redemption.

Our current status is one of chaos and danger. That is why Revelation 21–22 presents such an incredible solution to our current condition, because it is counterintuitive to what we know as the normative for human existence. God is, indeed, going to make His home with us and administer on earth the very life of heaven.

It is not just that God will apply the life of heaven to our world. Much more than that, He will bring heaven down to the earth! God the Son has already condescended to mankind in the incarnation to redeem mankind. That was when the purchase was made. Now, at the second coming, the kingdom of heaven will descend and permeate all of creation.

Heaven and earth will be joined as one, like a marriage between the two phenomena. Heaven and earth are two worlds waiting to become one. The transient journey of heaven (as it is right now) ends with the cosmic kiss of heaven and earth colliding by the power and will of God. There are two eternal marriages that will one day be consummated: one between heaven and the earth—forming a whole new creation; the other between Christ and the Church—forming a whole new relational intimacy. Note also the covenant language of Revelation 21:3. It is as if vows are being exchanged between God and mankind: "They will be His people, and God Himself will be with them as their God." Christ's first descension from heaven was to save people for God; His second descension from heaven will be to bring the life of heaven down to earth. Just as Christ intends to wed His people, He also intends to wed His two worlds.

The Death of Death

And he will wipe away every tear from their eyes, and death will not exist any longer, and mourning or wailing or pain will not exist any longer. The former things have passed away.

—Revelation 21:4

The last time I checked, unless we are referring to Enoch or Elijah, everyone who has lived has also died. Death is a dreadful thing. Ideally, no one would have to experience it. I have never met someone who isn't afraid of death. And for the rare few who don't fear death itself, they at least fear *dying*, hoping it to be a peaceful experience void of immense agony.

There is something so mysterious about "what comes next." I once was camping somewhere so dark that without a flashlight you couldn't see your own hand in front of you. That is how many people feel about death; it is a dark, unknown place in which we cannot see what is ahead of us. Francis Bacon was right: "Men fear death as children fear to go in the dark."

Christians should have a peculiar confidence toward death. Instead of fear, Christians can embrace death with immense joy, knowing that Jesus has promised eternal life to those who trust Him (John 11:25–26). Our resurrected King defeated death when He walked out of the grave. Not only is death defeated, it is "abolished," according to 2 Timothy 1:10.

While Jesus was certainly raised by God the Father, He also takes the credit for raising Himself from the dead. In John 2:19, Jesus speaks in the active voice in the Greek, meaning that He anticipated performing the action of raising Himself from the dead. Why does this matter? Because if we have a relationship with Jesus, then we don't have to be afraid of dying. We trust a worthy Savior who Himself conquered death on our behalf.

So, when God promises that "death shall be no more," we shouldn't have any problem believing this to be true. Jesus' resurrection is the proof that death has been rendered powerless. And one day, soon, death will die (Revelation 20:14).[101] Death will lay in a grave of its own. The graveyard will be vacant of its occupants.

The sorrow of death will become a memory of something that once was, but is no longer. Death will not merely be imprisoned and detained; it will be annihilated and destroyed. Thus, as Christians, we can embrace death as a valley we walk through, a passageway necessary to traverse in order to arrive at the shores of eternity.

Founders of various religions can make all sorts of audacious claims, but each of their bodies is dead in a grave somewhere. Only Christianity has a Savior who walked out of the grave, as He promised He would. Death could not hold Him; the grave could not contain Him. Acts 2:24 goes so far as to say "it was not possible" for death to keep Him down! Even the best of the best in boxing have times when they get knocked out by a punch—not our Lord and Savior.

Jesus experienced death. He *died*. And not just any death, He drank the cup of God's wrath on our behalf. And even that couldn't keep Him down. He was not meant to die to stay dead. Instead of merely His teachings living on after His death, He Himself lives on to rule and to reign from heaven right now, bringing history to its predetermined end and its new beginning.

In Isaiah 25:8, the prophet prophesies about the day when God would "swallow up death forever" and "wipe every tear from our eyes." Thinking about God personally wiping away the tears of our past pain is something so tremendous. We were not innocent in contributing to a world of sorrows. Many times, we contribute to the sorrow of others. But a day is coming when sorrow, mourning, pain, and ultimately death won't exist anymore.

I have met some people who have become too accustomed to the idea of death. If death feels like something so awful, so tragic, so out of place in this world, then good! Humanity was not created to die. First Corinthians 15:26 declares: "The ultimate enemy to be destroyed is death." And so it will be. The consequence and natural repercussion of all sin will cease, along with sin itself, never to repeat itself. Again, death is not natural. Death is the consequence and wage of sin—which is lethal. It is the destiny for those who never experience redemption; that is why the final judgment of the unredeemed is called the 'second death' (Revelation 20:6, 14; 21:8). Life is given as a gift of God's grace to participate in what only He inherits—immortal and eternal life.

All will be made right, and death will taste the permanent dose of its own medicine; death will die and there will be no resurrection for such a grotesque entity. And God Himself will be the One to wipe away our tears, comforting us with the knowledge that even suffering has an end, but joy will have a new birthday and God's life, love, and jubilee will have no end. This is a cause for elaborate celebration.

God with Man

It is hard to read the first four verses of Revelation 21 and not be amazed at how patient God has been in bringing salvation to people. We have just begun our look at the vision of the eternal state, but what we can gather so far is that God truly desires to dwell with us more intimately than the English language can convey.

At the grand finale of redemptive history, we see not man finding a way to dwell with God—no, we see God making His dwelling with man. His pursuit of us and toward us has been the story of the Bible since page one. The language in Revelation arises from the echoes of the Old Testament (Ezekiel 37:27; Leviticus 26:12).

There has never been a time when God has stopped pursuing us or when human effort has eclipsed the work of God to make a permanent home to live with each other. The triune God will one day delight in our company as we, and all the redeemed universe, will delight in His presence.

The Westminster Catechism speaks of the highest aim of humanity: "Man's chief end is to glorify God and enjoy Him forever." This implies a constant communion between the human and the divine presence. And God's manifold presence will be far more experiential than it is right now.

God's presence will be perfect (unveiled in quality), pervasive (comprehensive in scope), and permanent (eternal in duration). How God will love all His people so equally, collectively, and yet, individually is beyond me. But He is God and more than capable of flooding the new creation with His life, love, and presence—and that is enough for me to intellectually apprehend until I experience it myself.

The chronological journey of redemption of the creation of heaven and earth goes from being made, then marred, and then married. At the creation in Genesis 1, heaven and earth are made by God. After the Fall in Genesis 3, heaven and earth are marred by man's sin. And at the eschaton, heaven and earth will be married forever. All of creation will shout with joy as heaven and earth collide in a wedding of two worlds—a new creation.

Chapter 5 Questions

Main Truth: Heaven will descend to our sphere of reality and pervade all of the cosmos, providing us with God's dwelling and His life to transform our existence. Heaven and earth will become one, like a wedding that takes place between the two worlds—causing the abolition of death, decay, disease, and chaos.

Question: What is John's point in saying that there will be "no sea" in the new creation? What does this "sea-lessness" symbolize? Do you think this statement should be interpreted literally—why or why not?

_____

_____

_____

_____

_____

_____

_____

_____

_____

_____

_____

Question: Where is God's final dwelling? What does the "marriage" of heaven and earth mean?

_____

_____

_____

_____

_____

_____

_____

_____

_____

Question: Why can we have confidence in the ultimate

"death of death"? How should this inform our approach to death (either our own or that of our loved ones)?

_____

_____

_____

_____

_____

_____

_____

_____

_____

_____

_____

Action: Based on the scriptural truths highlighted in this chapter, write down some truthful and hopeful statements that you could share with someone who is grieving the death of a believer. How are the biblical promises about heaven far superior to the mythical platitudes that pervade our culture today?

Chapter Five Notes

CHAPTER SIX

God's Thesis Statement

He is the origin and goal of all history. He has the first
word in creation, and the last word, in new creation.[102]
—Richard Bauckham

Read: Revelation 21:5

When learning to write effectively, we must learn to
make a clear thesis statement. This tells the reader what
theme will encompass the entirety of the writing. All of
what is written is to contribute to the thesis, defending it,
explaining it, clarifying it, and so on.

In the case of the Bible, I would suggest that there is
one central theme through all the drama of the biblical
plot: new creation. In Genesis, we have the prototype of
creation—the first and original creation.[103] But as we saw
in chapter 1 of this book, this wasn't the final intended
destination for creation.

Everything in the Bible contributes to the thesis of new
creation: demonstrating the need, describing the process of

redemption, and promising the finished product of God's future work culminated. And because the Bible is God's story, He has both the first and the last word. He is the "author of life" (Acts 3:15 ESV). He is the Composer of the symphony of all of history.

The Thesis of Redemption

And the one seated on the throne said, "Behold, I am making all things new!" And he said, "Write, because these words are faithful and true."
—Revelation 21:5

In Revelation 21:5, the voice of God—the One who sits on the throne—calls out, "Behold, I am making all things new." This statement encompasses the very heart of the book of Revelation, and, I would venture to say, the very heart of the whole Bible. If you are looking for a thesis statement of God's redemptive work, look no further than Revelation 21:5.

The entire Bible can be summed up in these four words: creation, fall, redemption, culmination. All of these together describe an eschatological journey from first creation to "new creation."

When I was in high school, I tore the rotator cuff in my shoulder during a wrestling match. It took time and physical therapy, but eventually my shoulder was better. Now when I say it was "better," though, I mean it was better than when it was injured. I have surpassed the strength I had in high school, but I will never have the range of motion I once had in my right shoulder before the injury.

This would be a dissatisfying analogy to illustrate what God does with our horribly injured world (and even more injured humans in it). God does not take the bruised creation and put a Band-Aid over its wounds. He doesn't look upon our chronic illness (sin) and simply prescribe painkillers.

No, God takes this creation and *transforms* it into something so par-excellence that it is called "new"! Our very bodies and our minds—the totality of our being—will experience God's renewal in such a way that nothing else could even add to it. If God were to set out a "suggestions" e-mail box after He is finished with us, I promise you it would remain empty forever!

The other noteworthy quality of God's "new" creation is that it *stays* new and fresh. Reread Revelation 21:1–5. If the eternal God is dwelling with a creation worthy of His infinite glory, and the "former things," such as death and decay, have passed away, then there is no way that life in the eternal state will ever feel "old" or "rusty."

When we think of something new, our only concept is within the realm of perpetual decay. For example, the moment you drive a new car off the lot, it loses a portion of its value. Within hours of seeing the latest and greatest blockbuster movie, you are already looking forward to what you saw in the previews, because that is what will soon be new. And the day you turn fifty, you begin to fear your life is nearing its end.

The point is that we, not God, have the wrong category for what "new" really is. God will be the very Source and Sustainer of the constant newness of life that will mark life in the consummated creation.

The present tense ("I am making") does not refer to the *present time* of the Church age (now), but it enforces the certainty that the future new creation will occur. It is a "prophetic present,"[104] or a "futuristic present," in which the effects are inaugurated, but the culminated fulfillment remains primarily in the future. Osborne writes, "Today there is an inaugurated aspect to this: Every Christian is now a 'new creation' in preparation for the final 'new creation' in eternity."[105] Because God is (present tense) making all things new, our identity as a new creation is both a present reality and a future hope.

This book heavily emphasizes the hope we have in the future. However, I want to note that many New Testament passages do exhort us to live as new creations even now (cf. 2 Corinthians 5:17). God *is* making all things new. We will see it come to fruition in a spectacular way in the future, far beyond anything we see now, but that doesn't mean we should live as if we are stuck in a waiting room, bored and unable to make any sort of real impact for eternity.

In Jesus' incarnation, the life of heaven dwelled among us, providing points of intersection between the natural and the supernatural. In Christ, Christians—indwelled and empowered by the Holy Spirit—can live as God's new creation initiated in the world.

The way we live now should be so drastically different, so holy, so in awe of God that it is as if the very presence of God is always with us—after all, isn't that what we claim when we say that the Holy Spirit lives in us?

We have belabored the point that God's new, *kainos* creation will be superior in quality to what we have now.

Moreover, we have noted that there will be continuity and discontinuity to what we currently experience. But how should we make sense of all of this?

At this time, I lean into the eloquent genius of C.S. Lewis. In his concluding book to the Chronicles of Narnia series, *The Last Battle*, Lewis describes a scene in which Lucy, her family, and her friends are entering Aslan's country (representing heaven), and she begins her journey into the country, saddened to leave Narnia behind. What she sees next surprises both Lucy and the reader:

> "Those hills," said Lucy, "the nice woody ones and the blue ones behind—aren't they very like the southern border of Narnia."
>
> "Like!" cried Edmund after a moment's silence. "Why they're exactly like. Look, there's Mount Pire with his forked head, and there's the pass into Archenland and everything!"
>
> "And yet they're not like," said Lucy. "They're different. They have more colours on them and they look further away than I remembered and they're more...more...oh, I don't know..."
>
> "More like the real thing," said the Lord Digory softly.
>
> Suddenly Farsight the Eagle spread his wings, soared thirty or forty feet up into the air, circled round and then alighted on the ground.
>
> "Kings and Queens," he cried, "we have all been blind. We are only beginning to see where we are. From up there I have seen it all—Ettinsmuir, Beaversdam, the Great River, and Cair Paravel still shining on the edge of the Eastern Sea. Narnia is not dead. This is Narnia."
>
> "But how can it be?" said Peter. "For Aslan told us older

ones that we should never return to Narnia, and here we are."

"Yes," said Eustace. "And we saw it all destroyed and the sun put out."

"And it's all so different," said Lucy.

"The Eagle is right," said the Lord Digory. "Listen, Peter. When Aslan said you could never go back to Narnia, he meant the Narnia you were thinking of. But that was not the real Narnia. That had a beginning and an end. It was only a shadow or a copy of the real Narnia, which has always been here and always will be here: just as our own world, England and all, is only a shadow or copy of something in Aslan's real world."

The difference between the old Narnia and the new Narnia was like that. The new one was a deeper country: every rock and flower and blade of grass looked as if it meant more. I can't describe it any better than that: if you ever get there, you will know what I mean.

It was the Unicorn who summed up what everyone was feeling. He stamped his right forehoof on the ground and neighed and then cried:

"I have come home at last! This is my real country! I belong here. This is the land I have been looking for all my life, though I never knew it till now. The reason why we loved the old Narnia is that it sometimes looked a little like this."[106]

Lewis, brilliantly, in his Narnia series, calls our present world "the Shadowlands," because it foreshadows what is to come, but cannot completely preview its splendor. I think of Lewis's children's story as the best explanation I have ever heard of the simultaneous continuity and discontinuity between the current world and the new world to come. We will experience a world so perfect, we will no longer have ambitions greater than our reality; thus, we will be able to be perfectly present, never dreaming about a better life.

Excursus: A Theology of Resurrection Bodies

Within the continuity of things that are being made new is the biblical promise of resurrected, glorified, new bodies to accompany the new creation. God's redemption is holistic, making every fiber of our being new, from our hearts to our bodies.

As amazing as the human body is, we all live keenly aware of its deficiencies. We can be encouraged by what Scripture has to say about receiving a new, glorified body. There are three specific passages I want us to consider.

Romans 8:23 reads, "And not only creation, but we ourselves having the first fruits of the Spirit we even groan inwardly as we eagerly await for adoption as sons, the redemption of our bodies." This is found during Paul's argument as he persuades his readers that our present suffering is not comparable to the glorious future awaiting us (Romans 8:18).

This verse reminds us that even the goodness of God that we behold here and now is only a foretaste of what is to come—and part of that includes the redemption of our physical bodies.

In its original context, "redemption" was a word used when speaking of buying back or setting a slave free from his or her condition.[107] The ransom was the payment; redemption was the purchase, or the result. There is a sense that at the Fall, the true strength and potential of our bodies was forfeited by our succumbing to sin.

Again, I have argued for the importance of the physical. In our physicality, we can worship and enjoy God (remember my snorkeling example?). In fact, we cannot worship God to the utmost of our ability until we have bodies that will be capable of doing so.

Philippians 3:20–21 builds further on this idea: "But our citizenship is in heaven, and from it we await a Savior, the Lord Jesus Christ, who will transform our lowly body to be like his glorious body, by the power that enables him even to subject all things to himself" (ESV).

First, notice how we wait for Jesus to come back here, to our cosmos, rather than waiting to flee away from God's created universe. Christ our Savior will return to redeem the cosmos. Paul's theology of "glorified bodies" tells us that our future will never include a disembodied existence.

The Greek word behind "transformed" or "changed" is where we get the English concept of metamorphosis. In this transformation (literally: *trans* = to change; *form* = form/shape), we can view that our bodies are changed into the highest form and intention of human physical potential, as opposed to their current marred state. The key here is that they are *changed*, not *discarded*; there is both continuity and discontinuity in comparison to our present condition.

Our bodies will be "transformed" to the quality and likeness of none other than Christ's "glorious body." The splendor and radiance of Jesus' body will be ours, too. However, ours will only illuminate glory right back to the One who gave it to us. Jesus' glorified body is said to be "brighter than the sun" (Acts 26:13), and the saints' future bodies are said to be lumineers "like the stars" (Daniel 12:3).

Mark Keown writes in his commentary on Philippians, "Believers will have the same type of body as Christ, a spiritual body, 'a physical body renovated by the Spirit of Christ and therefore suited to heavenly immortality.'"[108] This is a fundamental motivator when we talk about enduring until the end.

First Corinthians 15 presents some of the best comprehensive New Testament treatment on a theology of the resurrection. Verses 12 through 34 speak as an apologetic to the veracity of Christ's resurrection and its implications for everything we believe, including our own future bodily resurrection.

Our resurrection bodies are called "heavenly bodies" (1 Corinthians 15:40). Verses 40–49 continue the contrast between the earthly and heavenly body juxtaposing dishonor and glory; weakness and power; natural and spiritual. The glorified body is sown in "power," in that it is physically superior. These bodies are "spiritual" in the sense of being Spirit-dominated.

They will be bodies completely filled by the Spirit of God; created new by the Spirit of God; given life by the Spirit of God; adapted to heavenly existence; controlled by the spirit; and in harmony with God's Spirit.[109]

These characteristics do not indicate immaterial bodies, but supernatural ones, ones that belong to the Spirit and the coming age, which is not limited by time and space, yet ones that are material.[110] The key here is not to fall into the trap of equating "spiritual" to "immaterial"; this would negate one of Paul's primary arguments in 1 Corinthians, especially in chapter 15.

The Greek word here is *pneumatikos*, which comes from the word *pneuma*, which is the word for "Spirit," as in the "Holy Spirit."[111] I am grateful to Wright's eloquent explanation on this point:

> Greek adjectives ending in -ikos, do not describe the material out of which things are made, but the power or energy which animates them. It is the difference between asking on the one hand "is this a wooden ship or an iron ship?" (the material from which it is made) and asking on the other "is this a steam ship or a sailing ship?" (the energy which empowers it). Paul is talking about the present body, which is animated by the normal human psychē (the life-force we all possess here and now, which gets us through the present life but is ultimately powerless against illness, injury, decay and death), and the future body which is animated by God's pneuma, God's breath of new life, the energizing power of God's new creation.[112]

This has everything to do with the theme of new creation. Our current body is part of the first things, while the resurrected body is of the last things. Paul is showing us the distinction between protology (the first Adam) and eschatology (Jesus, the last Adam).

Those who are in Christ, belonging to Him, reap the benefits exclusive to the Messianic King. Receiving the eschatological blessing is contingent upon the recipient being united to the Giver of the blessing; thus Jesus is the "life-giving Spirit" (1 Corinthians 15:45).[113]

The section ends with Paul saying with certainty that the believer will bear "the image of the heavenly man" (1

Corinthians 15:49). This juxtaposition affirms that even Adam's condition was incomplete in that it lacked eschatological finality. If the image of Adam is inferior to Christ (which, of course, it is), then we can infer that our glorified bodies will be superior to Adam and Eve's. It is difficult to know for certain how we will use our resurrection bodies. What are the activities of the new world? We are not given an itinerary. We can make educated inferences, but ultimately, we have to trust that God has for us a physical existence of purpose and delight far beyond what we could comprehend.

Hoekema describes it as thus: "We shall live to God's praise in glorified, resurrected bodies. On that new earth, therefore, we hope to spend eternity, enjoying its beauties, exploring its resources, and using its treasures to the glory of God."[114]

I also concur with Spurgeon's words on the topic:

Whatever are the characteristics of the Saviour's glorified body, they are to be the characteristics of your body also. You are to have an immortal body, a spiritual body, a body incapable of pain, and suffering, and decay, a body which shall be suited to your emancipated spirit, a body having a wider range than this limited earthly sphere, having greater powers of locomotion, perhaps flying, swiftly as light, from world to world, or possibly having the power even to outrun the lightning's flash. I do not know how wondrous Christ's glorified body is; but I do "know that, when he shall appear, we shall be like him (even in body); for we shall see him as he is" (1 John 3:2).[115]

If I were allowed to speculate beyond what is scripturally explicit, I would predict that our bodies won't be marked by physical limitations. Beyond lacking physical decay and frailty, I believe our glorified bodies will have a radiant beauty and physical abilities far beyond what they do now. Like Spurgeon, I do not think flying is out of question. I do not think hours and hours spent below water will be impossible (not that we will even measure time like we do now).

The key to understanding our future resurrection bodies is to look at Christ's resurrection. Something that was literally impossible has become possible, and even promised to believers, through the resurrection of the Lord Jesus. Through Christ's resurrection, the triune God is going to flood the entire creation—believers, planets, mountains, plants, etc.—with resurrection power, thus bringing glorious newness to everything.

Who Is the Alpha and the Omega?

And He said to me, "Everything is accomplished! I am the Alpha and the Omega, the beginning and the end."
—Revelation 21:6a

The speaker in Revelation 21:6 is the One on the throne, God the Father.[116] He declares Himself to be the "Alpha and the Omega," an unarguable title of deity. "Alpha" is the first letter in the Greek alphabet. "Omega," as you may have guessed, is the last letter. This unites creation and eschatology.

As Mitchell Reddish puts it in *Alpha and Omega*, "The God who brought the world into existence is the same one who will bring the world to completion.... In later rabbinic writings the first and last letters of the alphabet were used to denote something in its entirety…to describe God as the Alpha and the Omega is not a restriction of God to only the beginning and the end but is a declaration of the totality of God's power and control."[117]

I am the Alpha and the Omega, the first, and the last, the beginning and the end.
—Jesus in Revelation 22:13

It would be difficult to imagine a more explicit claim to deity. Jesus claims a triad of titles that are basically communicating the same thing; nevertheless, these titles are exclusive to describing God. So, if Jesus is claiming such titles, He is attributing Himself to participation in the Godhead.

"Alpha and Omega" was already spoken of the Father. So, by sharing an exact title with the Father, Jesus unites their ontological identity while remaining distinct in person from the Father. He is not a "second god"; He is the very same essence as God and shares in the eternal being of God.

In Revelation 1:17 and 2:8, Jesus refers to Himself as the "first and the last." This is a description of Yahweh rooted in Isaiah's writings.[118] Motyer writes, "As *first* he does not derive his being from any other, but is self-existing; as *last* he remains supreme at the End."[119]

Both God and Jesus are given titles that indicate they share in the same divine, eternal identity prior to creation. The triune God "has the first word, in creation, and the last word, in new creation,"[120] as Bauckham puts it.

The glory of God filling and satisfying all things in the new creation is the purpose of the first creation. In the eternal state filled with the glory of God, sin will be completely eradicated. Christ is the means for accomplishing redemption (the Lamb of God motif) and is the destiny of redemption (being the divine spouse of all the redeemed people). He is the Creator and the Consummator of all things, and to Him will be all the glory!

What Isn't in the New Creation?

But as for the cowards and unbelievers and detestable persons and murderers and sexually immoral people and sorcerers and idolaters and all liars, their share is in the lake that burns with fire and sulphur, which is the second death.

—Revelation 21:8

The eternal state is so perfect because the presence of sin has been banished permanently. If sin could exist in the new creation, it would be another fallen world, filled with fallen people.

God has decided to give us His assurance that this new world will not fall into the state of this present world. This means that not only sin, but those marked by sin without having been redeemed, will not be present in the new creation. The day sin ceases to exist, death will cease to exist also.

Part of the blessing of the new creation will be the fact that sin will no longer exist. Not only will sin's presence be banished externally, but it will also be gone internally. There will be no hint of unholiness within us.

Everything about us will be ethically purified, and thus every inhabitant of the new world will only contribute goodness to it. There will not be a speck of pollution from immorality or evil. We will have no temptation, no desire, to ever operate in a way that is antagonistic to God's design.

This list of sinners can make even the redeemed saint uncomfortable to read. Many Christians can easily associate with falling short and being guilty of some of the sins listed. The difference is what we are marked by; we are no longer characterized by the sins that once trapped us. Rather, we are covered by the blood of the Lamb.

As the Israelites once painted the blood of a lamb over the doors of their homes, we have also placed the Lamb of God's blood over our hearts. The basis of our refuge is the faithful intercession of Jesus, who is for us both the priest and the sacrifice. We are saved by our union with Christ, and it is our faith in Christ that joins our person to His. That is our confidence.

While the subject of the judgment of the unredeemed may be uncomfortable for us to engage, we must, for the sake of the lost, engage it in a meaningful way. Plus, how can we shy away from such a topic that is so interwoven throughout the book of Revelation? Consider the portions of Revelation we did not even have the time to cover (chapters 1–3; 6–20) and the frequency in which judgment of the unbeliever is a subject that cannot be avoided. Similar language is also found in Revelation 21:27 and 22:15.

We must trust in God's justice, how He administers it, and upon whom He administers it. All of what He will do at the eschaton is for the protection of His people and the glory of His name.

The good news is that God is patient and loving. He does not want any to perish but all to come to repentance (2 Peter 3:9). This should motivate our evangelism, but what should motivate us even more is not the punishment of not knowing God, but the blessing of knowing Him—and being known by Him.

The Father's Love for Us

> To the one who is thirsty I will give water from the spring of the water of life freely. The one who conquers will inherit these things, and I will be his God and he will be my son.
> —*Revelation 21:6b–7*

Here we are in grave need of deliverance from sin, for which we are all guilty (Romans 3:23). Yet the wealth of the richest man, or the works of the most virtuous man, cannot earn what God offers to us in Christ. It is solely a gift (Romans 3:24) for those who will give not their money, and not their deeds, but their trust unto God—He wants our very hearts.

Our souls are born with a thirst that cannot be quenched by natural means. We are created with a God-sized hole in our hearts that will only be an empty vacuum without Him. One hundred billion galaxies cannot satisfy what only God can.

Revelation 21:6b is a refreshing reminder that the fountain of life-giving water is accessible to us "without cost." The mistake most people make here is assuming that "without cost" means that it is cheap. Salvation is costly.

Oh, the cost to redeem the lost! Jesus gave Himself to be the price of our purchase. When Jesus says in Mark 10:45 that He gives His life as the "ransom" (Greek: *lutron*), He means to say that He is the payment—literally the "price" of our release.[121]

I want you to think about that the next time you are tempted to cheapen God's grace for you. It may be offered to you as a gift, without any cost to you, but it was certainly not without cost to God. Praise be to the Lamb of God, who loves us and has ransomed us by His bloodshed sacrifice (Revelation 1:5).

The language of the "prevailer" is the same verbiage in the letters to the churches (Revelation chapters 2–3).[122] This is the victorious description of those who maintain allegiance to King Jesus despite the hostility of the fallen world.

Believers will receive all the eschatological promises of God. This encourages us that our endurance is not in vain; there is indeed a great inheritance coming if we press on, "prevailing" by trusting the Lamb (Revelation 12:11).

By being united to Christ through faith, we are heirs according to the promise (Galatians 3:26–29). These blessings culminate in the realization of the two highest relational roles—receiving Christ as the divine spouse and receiving God as Father.

In view here is the blessed relationship we receive in relation to the Father. We become sons and daughters of God. The inheritance we receive is nothing less than the privileged inheritance of the eternal Son of God.[118]

To be "in Christ"[124] marks a spatial union in which our person is encapsulated by Christ's person. I like to illustrate what it means to be in Christ this way: If you are in the ocean, submerged and basking in the water, you partake of the benefits of being in the ocean, like the health benefits of the salt water on your skin. But you can only have these benefits if you are immersed in the ocean. In a similar sense, you can only partake of the benefits and blessings of God if you are in Jesus—immersed and engulfed in Him.

What is true of Jesus becomes true of us, because we are "in" Him. "Christ is still God's unique, divine son," as G.K. Beale notes, "but those whom he represents receive the privileges of his sonship."[125]

Perhaps the most difficult truth to grasp about our union with Christ and the sonship (and daughtership) we receive is the boundless love that is given to us. In Christ, we become the very object of God's divine love. It is not a comparison of whom God the Father loves more, Jesus or us; His affection for us is equal.

I am going to make this personal to you. Assuming you have placed your trust in Jesus as a believer, the Father's love for you is rooted in and secure in His love for Jesus. This means that the Father loves you as much as He loves Jesus, because you are *in* Jesus.

We have probably heard it said many times, that "God loves you." But do you understand what that means? Can you fathom how much that is true? Have you ever, just for one evening, slowed down the pace of your busy mind and tried to dwell on that thought?

The life we have in the Son of God is the life that He shares with the Father in the unity of the Spirit. We are welcomed into the life and love of the Trinity by God's abundant grace lavished upon us. God's economic love comes from the love that is His very ontology. And to say the same thing in lay terms, God loves you with the very same love with which He loves Himself. The love shared between the Father, Son, and Spirit is shared with you and me, who are *in* Jesus.

D.A. Carson explains, "Christians themselves have been caught up into the love of the Father for the Son, secure and content and fulfilled because [believers are] loved by the Almighty himself (*cf.* Ephesians 3:17b–19), with the very same love he reserves for his Son. It is hard to imagine a more compelling evangelistic appeal."[126]

The reality is, you cannot speak too highly of love that comes from an infinite God. There is no vocabulary that can express or put a cap on the love the Father has for His Son and for those who are in His Son and are now and forevermore His sons and daughters. Words simply fail to do justice to such a thing. In the present age, our feelings are still marred by sin, and the "feeling" comes and goes. But God's love doesn't shift or change; it is constant even when our feelings aren't.

We currently have an imperfect experience of a perfect reality that we really are sons and daughters of God in Christ. However, one day our experience will be perfectly in correlation with that reality. We will finally, fully, and forever experience the love of the Father for us as His kids. That is a hope worth the wait. That is a hope worth inviting others into.

WORKBOOK

Chapter 6 Questions

Main Truth: God's thesis statement since the beginning has been: "Behold, I am making all things new." We can begin to experience this today and look forward to the culmination of His new cosmic redemption.

Question: How do you see God's "thesis statement" repeated throughout the entire Bible?

_____

_____

_____

_____

_____

_____

_____

Question: In what ways will our physical resurrection bodies be different from our current bodies? What do we know about this from Scripture? What do you imagine our resurrection bodies will be like?

Question: "The Father loves you as much as He loves Jesus because you are in Jesus." How would your life change if you lived daily believing and acting upon this truth?

_____

_____

_____

_____

_____

_____

_____

_____

_____

_____

Action: Considering what you have learned, take time to evaluate how you are doing in sharing your faith. If you have ever done personal evangelism training, review what you learned. If not, talk to your pastor about how you can become better equipped to share the Gospel. Ask God for new and consistent opportunities to share your faith with family, friends, and those in the community who need Him.

Chapter Six Notes

CHAPTER SEVEN

The Most Holy Place

The enjoyment of God is the only happiness with which our souls can be satisfied...Fathers and mothers, husbands, wives, or children, or the company of earthly friends. These are but shadows; but the enjoyment of God is the substance. These are but scattered beams; but God is the sun. These are but streams; but God is the fountain. These are but drops, but God is the ocean.[127]

—Jonathan Edwards

Read: Revelation 21:9–27

The sun's rays are good for us, in moderation of course. Healthy amounts of exposure to the sun allow us to receive vitamin D, which helps us absorb the calcium that is essential for healthy bones.

Not only that, but the sun's rays can enhance people's moods, thus decreasing symptoms of depression. The chemical that is produced from sun exposure can even help prevent various sorts of cancer! I am lucky to live in *Sun*-Diego (that is, San Diego, California), where we get plenty of sunshine.

However, we must also be cautious not to overstay our welcome exposed to the sun's rays. It is recommended that if you plan on being exposed to sunlight beyond fifteen minutes, you wear some type of sunscreen. Too much sun and we can greatly increase our chances of skin cancer.

When we get sunburned, the DNA in our cells is damaged. Too much sun can harm our immune systems. And staring directly at the sun when it is at full strength can potentially blind us. So, in summary, the sun's rays are both necessary for our health, but also potentially dangerous. All of this information provides a helpful illustration for us.

To be in God's presence is the very quintessence of life itself. Created in the image of God, we are made to be completely dependent upon Him. Psalm 16:11 even tells us that in God's presence is the "fullness of joy." The word used for "fullness" here denotes total satisfaction.

Our triune God is good; He is the Giver and Sustainer of life. However, He is also holy and absolutely devoid of all sin. Interestingly enough, God's presence is both immanent and transcendent. In other words, God is both present in His creation but also separate from His creation. The world is gifted with His presence, but not in its entirety. God's presence is both fundamental and fatal to us.

Like our experience with the sun's rays, we absolutely need exposure to God's presence, but unfortunately, with the reality of sin in our lives, we cannot be in God's full presence. A sinful person cannot stand in the full glory of God's presence; that person would be obliterated by God's powerful, dangerous, and fatal presence—His holiness.

This chapter will lead us to discover, as we already have begun to see, that the new Jerusalem is a sacred place where God's presence will be unveiled to us and will bless us instead of harming us.

The New Jerusalem: A People and a Place

And one of the seven angels who had the seven bowls full of the seven last plagues came and spoke with me, saying, "Come, I will show you the bride, the wife of the Lamb." And he carried me away in the Spirit to a great and lofty mountain, and showed me the holy city, Jerusalem, coming down out of heaven from God, that has the glory of God. Its radiance is like a precious stone, something like a jasper stone, shining like crystal. It has a great and high wall that has twelve gates, and at the gates twelve angels, and names written on the gates which are of the twelve tribes of the sons of Israel—on the east, three gates, and on the north, three gates, and on the south, three gates, and on the west, three gates. And the wall of the city has twelve foundations, and on them are twelve names of the twelve apostles of the Lamb.

—Revelation 21:9–14

It is easy to get confused when reading this passage. There seems to be a mixed use of metaphors again. How is the bride of the Lamb now a city that is descending out of heaven? It appears that the heavenly city is both a people (the bride of Christ) and a place (the new Jerusalem).

The "new Jerusalem" is referenced back in Revelation 3:12, where all believers (the "prevailers") obtain the inheritance within the "new Jerusalem." Jesus states in that same verse that this city will come down from heaven. This matches the description of what will happen according to Revelation 21:2. This idea is not foreign to the rest of the Bible; once again, most imagery in Revelation is rooted in something promised in the Old Testament.

Isaiah 65:17 contains one of first announcements of the future promised new heavens and new earth. In verse 18, God says, "I *am* about to create Jerusalem *as a source of* rejoicing, and her people *as a source of* joy" (emphasis mine). Dwell on that: God is making a place and a people to be marked by happiness!

I like how Ortlund and Hughes describe it: "In the end, [according to Isaiah 65:18] there will be only one commandment for God's servants to obey forever and ever: 'Be glad and rejoice forever in that which I create.'"[128]

Continuing the thought in Isaiah 65, in verse 19, God says, "I will shout in exultation over Jerusalem, and I will rejoice over my people." It is not hard to imagine that we could celebrate with sheer delight what God has done and will do, but to think that God will rejoice in *us*? It almost sounds absurd! How can we bring any pleasure to the Lord? This shouldn't puff us up or make us think highly of ourselves. Instead, it should show us how great God is, that He would take delight in us.

The relationship between God and His people is mutual in the common joy shared; however, this is only due to the redemptive work of God. All of our blessing comes from God as the divine Blesser. He receives all the credit and all the glory for all the good that will be ours to receive as the people of God.

We are establishing that the new Jerusalem is a city, but this city is both a people and a place. Osborne says, "The new Jerusalem is not only a place but also a people. The city of God is the place where the saints will live for eternity, yet it is wholly composed of the people themselves."[129]

As a people, the new Jerusalem is God's collective community of redeemed people brought forth from every tribe, nation, and tongue (Revelation 7:1–9). Gentiles (those of non-Jewish origin) are welcomed into God's covenant family through faith. It is as Paul says in Galatians 3:7: "...it is those of faith who are the sons of Abraham." And then in Galatians 3:9: "So then, those who are of faith are blessed along with Abraham, the man of faith."

The end of Paul's letter concludes by calling all believers the "Israel of God" (Galatians 6:16), authenticating that salvation is not based on ethnic origin (race), but on faith in Jesus (grace). This helps us not to become trapped into thinking of the new Jerusalem as exclusionary to non-Jewish people, for it has nothing to do with ethnicity.

Thus "as a place, the New Jerusalem is at once paradise, holy city, and temple. As paradise it is the natural world in its ideal state...as holy city, it fulfills the ideals of the ancient city, as the place where heaven and earth meet at the center of the earth...in which people live in ideal theocentric community...as temple, it is the place of God's immediate presence."[130]

All throughout Revelation, Jewish terminology is used to speak both of God's redeemed people from all over the globe, and of God's eschatological promises, maintaining a sort of continuity between the old and new covenants. We must remember that the first Christians (accurately) saw themselves as the fulfillment of Judaism in Christ.

This should make us comfortable in embracing the Jewish language in Revelation, and elsewhere in the Bible, because as Christians we are the true recipients of the promises of God, since Christ is the single beneficiary of all the promises.[131]

The vision includes a brief but important allusion to God's "mountain" (Revelation 21:10). Humans have always viewed mountaintops as places to aspire to reach. Both innate in humans and in biblical language, mountains play a special role in eschatology. Ever since Moses visited Mount Sinai, mountains have been associated with the presence of God.

In the ancient Near East, worldly temples were preferably built on the highest place topographically available, so they would be closer to heaven.[132] This indicated the symbolism of ascension, or heights, pertaining to the nearness to God and His heavenly abode.

Jewish literature anticipated that God's eventual mountain dwelling place would be on "the highest of the mountains" (Isaiah 2:2). This corresponds with what Ezekiel saw when he saw the new temple (Ezekiel 40:2), which he had to be transported to a "very high mountain" to see.

In the words of Ressegeie, the mountain is a "place where heaven and earth meet."[133] Where the tops of mountains literally begin to penetrate the atmosphere (or "heaven," by one of its meanings), the new Jerusalem descends upon the heights of mountains (showing that the city comes *to* us, *not* from *within* us), and suddenly the "place where heaven and earth meet" becomes the vantage point to watch in awe as cosmic renewal happens before

John's very eyes.

This agrees with the conclusion of our previous chapters, in which heaven, as God's reality, permeates our reality and provides eschatological fresh life to all the cosmos.

Revelation 21:11 draws special attention to jasper, which is emblematic of the glory of God. As we saw back in Revelation 4:3, this stone was mentioned to describe the appearance of the One sitting on the throne of heaven. Jasper, like the diamond, is clear, transparent, and brilliantly bright.

The meaning here communicates much about the future glory of the Church. Richard Brooks writes, "The glory of God is at last imparted to the glorified church and thoroughly reflected in her.... The church is adorned with the glory of God, radiated with it, filled with it—aglow with it!"[134]

The city shines with the radiance of the glory of God's presence. And all the inhabitants of the city shine because they are captivated by the light of the Lord of glory. "The Lord of glory," Dennis Johnson exults, "indwells his people and floods his new community with the beauty of his holiness."[135] The radiance of the city is nothing less than the outward beauty of infinite joy secured forevermore.

The foundation of the city, with the names of the "twelve apostles of the Lamb," reminds us of the temple vision in Ezekiel 48:30–35, where the twelve tribes are mentioned.

What could possibly be going on here? In a brilliant Old Testament allusion, John is showing us that the grand vision from Ezekiel includes the Old and New Covenant believers.

God's Global Temple

And the one who spoke with me was holding a golden measuring rod in order that he could measure the city and its gates and its wall. And the city is laid out as a square, and its length is the same as its width. And he measured the city with the measuring rod at twelve thousand stadia; the length and the width and the height of it are equal. And he measured its wall, one hundred forty-four cubits according to human measure, which is the angel's. And the material of its wall is jasper, and the city is pure gold, similar in appearance to pure glass. The foundations of the wall of the city are adorned with every kind of precious stone: the first foundation jasper, the second sapphire, the third chalcedony, the fourth emerald, the fifth sardonyx, the sixth carnelian, the seventh chrysolite, the eighth beryl, the ninth topaz, the tenth chrysoprase, the eleventh jacinth, the twelfth amethyst. And the twelve gates are twelve pearls, each one of the gates was from a single pearl. And the street of the city is pure gold, like transparent glass.

And I did not see a temple in it, for the Lord God All-Powerful is its temple, and the Lamb.
—Revelation 21:15–22

The stones mentioned in Revelation 21 are not arbitrary; John was not only seeing something, but he was communicating something to his audience. Jewish high priests would wear two onyx stones on their shoulders. All of the twelve tribes of Israel were named on them, six names on each stone (Exodus 28:9–12).

The breastplate of the high priest was a memorial, and these stones served the purpose of remembrance. But what were they remembering? Eden. According to Ezekiel

28:13, onyx was a stone that was found in the garden of God.

It was last seen in Eden, but where else will we see it? On the foundations of the walls of the New Jerusalem, in the new Eden (Revelation 21:20). David Chilton says, "The onyx stones on the high priest's shoulders served to remind the people of Eden, the perfect Earth that should be kept alive in the hearts, dreams, and hopes of God's people."[136]

God intentionally had the high priest, as His representative for His people, wear what symbolized the very land they had lost but looked to regain—paradise. The Lord encouraged His people with a memorial stone of the past, pointing them toward their promised future.

The measurements of the holy city formed a perfect cube. This is not to say that the city is a literal cube. John's audience would have recognized what the measurements were describing—the holy of holies.

In Exodus, we learn that God allowed Moses to dwell in His presence in a unique way, unlike the rest of Israel. At one point, Moses's face even radiated as he left Mount Sinai and went back to the Israelites.

Moses learned that God planned to have His presence with His people dwell in a mysterious tabernacle. Moses received the pattern, and Aaron became the first official high priest over Israel.

Hundreds of years later, the prophet Ezekiel was taken up to the high mountain of the Lord, and an angel with a measuring rod showed him the dimensions for God's new temple (Ezekiel 40:1–4).

Like the description given in the book of Revelation,

the physical dimensions that were shown had symbolic meaning behind them. Both in the tabernacle during Moses's time and in the temple Solomon built, there was only one extra-special space shaped like a cube—the holy of holies, which sometimes was referred to as the "most holy place."[137]

Revelation mentions a measuring rod of "twelve thousand stadia" (Revelation 21:16). Like many parts of this apocalypse, this measurement is not to be taken literally, but it shows that the city is massive,[138] according to Beale's commentary on Revelation.

The city would be about 1,500 miles, which would cover the entire Mediterranean world, the size of the known world at the time, from Jerusalem to Spain. We see that God's temple is global in size, large enough to include *all* of the redeemed from every generation and every nation. (Who knows? Maybe the new world will even be much larger than the current one. I trust population will not be a problem for God to handle.)

Both the tabernacle and the temple in the Old Testament were faint previews of the eventual, eternal dwelling place of the Lord with His people.[139] The temple represented God's presence with His people, but in the eternal state the whole new creation will be a temple. Further, God and the Lamb will be the temple (Revelation 21:22). Intriguingly, in other passages, believers are called God's temple (1 Corinthians 3:16–17).

What do we make of all of this? God's presence won't be "in heaven," for heaven will be one with the earth. God's presence won't be restricted to a veiled room within the temple, for the entire new creation will be capable of enjoying the unveiled, sacred presence of God. This is something a Jew could only have dreamed of.

If you read 1 Kings 6–8 (which contains the building of the temple by King Solomon) in its entirety, you will notice a few things; chief among those would be Solomon's hope to have the temple be a place of prayer.

What is prayer, but the communication between the God and man? Prayer recognizes God's immanence among us (He hears us, and thus He is in a sense present among us), while acknowledging His transcendence far beyond us (He is in heaven and we are yet on the earth).

The tabernacle and then the temple were viewed as a model, or a microcosm, of the cosmos. To summarize a preeminent purpose of the temple from an Old Testament perspective, I would say this: The purpose of the temple was to be a place of intersection between God and man; heaven and earth; life above and life below. In other words, the temple acted as a place of mediation between God and His people.

N.T. Wright comments:

> We must remind ourselves that, for the Jews, the Temple was where the one true God had promised to make his home. The Temple was the place where heaven and earth were joined together. It was the place you went to meet with God. It was the place of sacrifice, of atonement, the place where you went for festivals because you went to celebrate the presence and love of God.[140]

No Need for a Temple

So, the means of mediation has been replaced, as the

Lamb has taken the Church as His bride, whom He sacrificed Himself to redeem. Thus, no more mediation is needed, because the sacrificial ceremony has been eclipsed by the greatest wedding ceremony of all time.

Temples will no longer be needed, because the reality of the temple's true meaning has arrived. Wright says, "The Temple in Jerusalem was always designed, it seems, as a pointer to, and an advance symbol for, the presence of God himself. When the reality is there, the signpost is no longer necessary."[141]

God and the Lamb become the realization of all that was symbolized by the temple. The shadow has faded in the background as the substance has appeared.

Arguably, temples have already faded into the background, as the people of God, the Church, are ambassadors of God as His temple presence in the world. However, the inaugurated temple presence through the Church still awaits the consummated presence of God.

God's presence will be pervasive in scope, permanent in duration, and perfect in quality—blessing all of creation in an uncanny way unlike any other time in all of history. The glorious presence of the triune God will be, simultaneously, with us, indwelling us, and all around us.

Meredith Kline summarizes this, saying, "By virtue of this union of the new heaven and new earth, the earth is 'heavenized.' The new earth is the focal site of the enthroned triune Presence, the center of a cosmic holy of holies (cf. Revelation 11:19; 21:16)."[142]

We know that John's vision is showing us not just the city being like a temple, but also like the most holy place of the temple, the holy of holies, because the street of the city is "pure gold, like transparent glass" (Revelation 21:21b). While our modern culture has retained the precious value of gold, we tend to think of it strictly in its monetary value or its aesthetic splendor.

However, 2 Chronicles 3:8 describes the appearance of the holy of holies as being overlaid "with six hundred talents of fine gold." That is approximately twenty-three tons of gold! But Solomon didn't stop there; the whole temple had drapings and coverings made of gold.[143]

For ancient Jews, hearing about streets of gold would make them think back to the temple of Solomon, and more specifically, to the holy of holies. Walking on gold was an entitlement of the high priest alone. So, for the whole city to be filled with streets of gold implies that the citizens would *all* be royal priests who would have the privilege and pleasure to serve and worship God.

How exactly will this look in the life of the new creation? We can only speculate. But the fact is that our eternal dwelling will be in the holy of holies![144] As golden cubes, the holy of holies and the new Jerusalem are clearly connected, the latter describing the fulfillment of the former. Beale states, "God's special presence, formerly limited to the holy of holies, has now extended out to encompass the entire visible heavens and the whole earth, which the holy place and the court respectively symbolized."[145] And since the temple was always a microcosm of the whole universe, the descriptive imagery of the city in Revelation 21 is actually transcendent in describing the condition of the entire new creation.

When Ariana and I were engaged, we lived many miles apart. I was in Washington and she was in San Diego. We utilized technology to talk on the phone every night. But now that we are married and together, it would be silly for me to call her on her cell phone every night. She is usually lying right next to me! Our nightly phone calls were good at that time, and they served as a temporary placeholder until we got to be fully present with each other. But now that we are together, there is no need for that anymore!

Likewise, and much more, why would we settle for God's veiled presence in the temple when we can be forever satisfied in a new world that, all of it, is God's manifest presence! It is not that there won't be a temple; instead, the entire world will be the temple, because our Triune God will be the temple!

You won't go to God's temple to worship. Everywhere will be sacred space. And everything you do will be an act of worship. Enjoying God and enjoying God's new creation world will be worship. If you think worship is limited to strictly singing songs, then you are missing the point. Worship is not just a song we sing; it is a lifestyle we live.

Bruce Milne wrote, "To live in this city is to live continually in the presence of the unveiled glory of God."[146] When something is veiled, it is concealed. Think of the lifting of the bride's veil by a groom, symbolizing the privilege he has gained into a type of intimacy that was once forbidden.

When I proposed to my wife, Ariana, I saw her as the most beautiful woman I have ever seen (and I still do). Honestly, it was, of course, her inward beauty that grappled my heart into loving her the way I do, but her outward beauty has still been part of many breathtaking memories. The New Jerusalem in Revelation 21:18–21 is described with precious stones, stones that were of immense value in the ancient world due to their appearance and characteristics. This takes us back to Revelation 4, in which God's appearance and throne are described in a similar sense. It thus becomes true that the heavenly city "has the glory of God."

The brilliance of God is now shared with His saints as a special possession and privilege. While outward human beauty does not assume inward beauty, God's beauty is not a façade. Any outward beauty of God stems from His inward holiness, which can only radiate what is absolutely pleasant to the eye.

City of Light

And the city has no need of the sun or of the moon, that they shine on it, for the glory of God illuminates it, and its lamp is the Lamb. And the nations will walk by its light, and the kings of the earth will bring their glory into it. And its gates will never be shut by day (for there will be no night there), and they will bring the glory and the honor of the nations into it. And every unclean thing and one who practices detestable things and falsehood will never enter into it, except those who are written in the book of life of the Lamb.
—Revelation 21:23-27

You may not know the name Vincent van Gogh, but you probably would recognize his famous painting *The Starry Night*. Van Gogh used a bright yellow in his paintings to symbolize the presence of God. In this particular painting, he filled the sky with big yellow circles, almost drawn in a spiral. But something else is fascinating about this painting.

Van Gogh situated a church building in the village below, but no light comes from its windows. However, you can notice the light present in the homes of the village, showing that God's presence dwells in the community of people, not in a church building.

One could also conclude that God's creation, both in the physical universe and in His human creatures, reflects the divine light. Van Gogh's use of yellow light to demonstrate the divine is not wrong at all. The biblical imagery of light calls for a study all its own, but the concept is certainly applicable to these verses, as well.

Revelation 21:23–27 appears to be a fulfillment of what had been promised back in Isaiah 60, specifically verses 1–3 and 19–20.

Arise, shine! For your light has come, and the glory of Yahweh has risen on you. For look! darkness shall cover the earth, and thick darkness the peoples, but Yahweh will rise on you, and his glory will appear over you. And nations shall come to your light, and kings to the bright light of your sunrise...

The sun shall no longer be your light by day, and for bright light the moon shall not give you light, but Yahweh will be your everlasting light, and your God your glory. Your sun shall no longer go down, and your moon shall not wane, for Yahweh himself will be your everlasting light, and your days of mourning shall come to an end.
—Isaiah 60:1–3, 19–20

This Old Testament picture envisions God's glory eclipsing any glory we can find in the universe. As big as the sun is, God is bigger. As radiant as the sun is, God is brighter. As effective as the sun's rays are in altering us when we are exposed to them, exposure to God's glory is even more transformative.

Like Moses's face being changed and literally glowing when he encountered the mere "back" side of God's glory,[147] so also the concept of encountering God's glory implies that the recipient will be changed by the glory and then naturally reflect it outward.[148] The New Jerusalem, being both a people and a place (a bride-city), is engulfed in the glory of God.

His light, like a lamp with a bulb inside of it, will indwell us and illuminate us. We will indeed shine with a physical glory that will match our inner glorification. This seems fitting of biblical figures with heavenly bodies, since angels who appear to people did appear to be clothed in light (Acts 12:7; Luke 2:9).

Moreover, as we have already discussed, our resurrection bodies are modeled after Christ's glorified body, and His body appears in majestic light, as when He confronted Paul on the Damascus road (Acts 9:3) and in the book of Revelation (1:16; 21:23).

It appears that Revelation's usage of "light" in this passage, similar to Isaiah's, carries both physical and illustrative meaning. This is what makes apocalyptic literature both difficult and exciting: Where does the symbolism end and the literalism begin?

There is a sense in which God's glory does act as a lumineer; however, it also acts as a transformative agent. This is not to say that the new creation won't have stars, moons, etc. That isn't the point of the text. The text doesn't negate the existence of these things, but rather shows the triune God's majestic superiority over these things. If these things will exist, they will be superfluous in comparison to the glory of God.

✳ It is worth mentioning that in the ancient world, darkness was seen as a covering for all kinds of evil to take place. Saying that there will be an absence of night serves to articulate the point that evil will no longer have a covering because it will be fully exposed and done away with. Robbers would even attack those on a road under the cover of the dark night sky. This is another way that the darkness and light motif plays into how we understand Revelation in its apocalyptic setting. Thus, the absence of the night is the absence of evil and danger.↯

I lean toward embracing the idea that the galaxies will indeed have stars and all sorts of luminaries. However, I am captivated by the fact that—instead of chasing the pinnacle of astronomy here and now as solar eclipses, meteor showers, and such—we will get to look upon God Himself, and His light will be infinitely more glorious and satisfying.

The New Jerusalem has no need of a sun or a moon because "the glory of God illuminates it." Isaiah 60:19–20 told of this coming day, when the Lord would be our "everlasting light," and when "our days of mourning shall come to an end." This fits the biblical theme of "light" being just as much about eschatological victory prevailing over the forces and effects of "darkness" (sin) as it is about literal radiance.

In John's writings,[149] the usage of light conveys multiple things about God: His holy purity (1 John 1:5, 7), His salvation (1 John 1:8), and His glory (Revelation 21:23). Believers are encouraged to "walk in the light" (1 John 1:5–7) since they belong to God, or to "the light." Jesus even declares Himself to be the "light of the world" (John 8:12). While much can be said about all of these verses, it is preeminent to remember that light symbolizes the presence of God and His transformative power over the domain of darkness.

When you study the physics of light, you will discover how pervasive light is. When darkness is met by light, darkness flees and light conquers. John 1:4 tells us that in Jesus is light. Christians embody the light of their Savior as they radiate and prevail over the surrounding darkness.

Verse 5 goes on to comfort us, saying that the "light shines in the darkness, and the darkness did not overcome it." Jesus is the "bright morning star" (Revelation 22:16), who secures victory over darkness and brings about a new day—bringing forth the city of light. The cosmos after the eschaton will only have light. That, I believe, is the emphasis of this passage—not some absence of stars in the heavens, but the triumph of the light over the forces of darkness.

> A bright light will shine to all the ends of the earth; many nations will come to you from far away, the inhabitants of the remotest parts of the earth to your holy name, bearing gifts in their hands for the King of heaven. Generation after generation will give joyful praise in you; the name of the chosen city will endure forever.[150]

Why would the city need a wall if God's enemies have

all been destroyed? Instead of preventing outsiders from coming in, the walls denote total security. It is not that the new world will have walls boxing us in, to restrain us or to protect us from potential evil, for there won't be any more evil. No, instead the walls are emblematic of being safe and sound under the protection of God's providential care. They indicate a refuge.

John's apocalypse does not shy away from the warnings of the impending judgment that is coming. Whenever hope is presented, it seems that a warning is, as well. Because only light will pervade the New Jerusalem, those who walk in darkness will have to accept their fate and live in darkness outside the gates of the heavenly city.

Their destruction will be their end. It is a sober warning to all readers to consider their current status and possibly begin a new life in the Messiah, trusting in Him as their Savior.

Excursus: Infinitely Happy in an Infinitely Happy God

The puritan John Whitlock once said, "This is the Christian's way and his end, his way is holiness, his end—happiness."

I cannot reiterate the sheer happiness that should exude from every believer as we cherish the joy of our salvation and the coming of its full benefits. To my mind, it is so unfortunate when Christians say something like, "God does not want us to be happy; He wants us to be holy." This frustrates me, because it makes it sound like holiness and happiness are inherently at odds with one another.

As I study the Bible, I become more and more convinced that the way of holiness is the way of happiness. I hope I have been successful thus far in presenting the idea that the coming new creation is one of *both* holiness and happiness—to their fullest potential.

And yet, we still have more to unpack, more that should make your heart leap with joy as we consider the grace of God. But don't just take my word for it! I want to share a few thoughts from other noteworthy believers about the intrinsic relationship between holiness and happiness.

Charles Spurgeon, the "prince of preachers," spoke these words concerning John 15:11: "A Christian has never fully realized what Christ came to make him until he has grasped the joy of the Lord. Christ wishes his people to be happy. When they are perfect, as he will make them in due time, they shall also be perfectly happy. As heaven is the place of pure holiness, so is it the place of unalloyed happiness; and in proportion as we get ready for heaven, we shall have some of the joy which belongs to heaven, and it is our Saviour's will that even now his joy should remain in us, and that our joy should be full."[151]

Spurgeon, on a different occasion, said, "Many people seem to think that it is a very sorrowful thing to be a Christian, that believers in Christ are a miserable, unhappy lot of folk who never enjoy themselves.... *We serve a happy God,* and we believe in a joyous gospel, and the love of Christ in our hearts has made us anticipate many of the joys of heaven even while we are here on earth."[152]

Have you ever considered the idea that God is a happy God? If we do not believe this truth about God, then we are training ourselves, and others, to believe that if we want holiness, we must go to God, but if we want happiness, we need to run the opposite direction.

Do you see the danger in this? We must believe that God is happy and the source of happiness; otherwise we will flee to somewhere or someone else for our heart's delight. I would even argue that among the attributes of God is the very attribute of happiness.

Spurgeon preached over five hundred times about the intimate relationship between holiness and happiness: "One great part of the joy of the glorified will be the perfection of their characters, for he that is holy must be happy. Perfection of holiness must mean perfection of happiness, the two things must go together. Sin and sorrow cannot be divorced, and holiness and happiness cannot be separated."[153]

I am not saying that we should define happiness the same way the fallen world does. Our culture has definitions of love, peace, and happiness that are all much different from that of Scripture. The joy of the Lord I speak of is an indestructible joy.

Spurgeon also wrote, "Believers are not dependent upon circumstances. Their joy comes not from what they have, but from what they are; not from where they are, but from whose they are."[154]

We must never underestimate the quality of worship that comes from a happy heart.

Whether I am conscious of it or not, I glorify the Taco Stand[155] whenever I eat there. I enjoy every bite and I tell everyone I know that it is the best taco shop I have ever been to. Of course, I do not worship tacos or any other food I enjoy. I worship God, and I recognize that any holy pleasure granted to me is, as Jonathan Edwards said, only "but streams; but God is the fountain." God is the source of all happiness. Any joy I receive should lead me to God, and in Him I can be totally immersed in divine happiness and dive into the infinite depths of His joy.

Jesus, in John 15:11, said, "I have spoken these things to you in order that my joy may be in you, and your joy may be made complete." This verse tells us that Jesus wants to give us the very joy that He Himself possesses and that He wishes our joy would be full. Not a "cup half full," but a cup full! Not full of fleeting joy, but full of the joy of the Lord, the very joy of Jesus!

Do we believe His words? We forget that one of the reasons Jesus came was to secure for us an indestructible joy. And have we forgotten that one of the fruit of the Spirit is joy (Galatians 5:22–23)? That means that a natural byproduct of God's Spirit at work in our lives results in joy! Isaac Watts, the hymnwriter of the timeless "Joy to the World," said it best: "Religion was never designed to make our pleasures less."

The new creation will be a place of infinite, eternal happiness because of God's presence. The ancient context of God's presence being a "blessing" is literally God's presence "happifying"[156] the recipients. Graham and De Lancey call heaven "the happifying Presence of the glorious God."[157]

So, when all of creation will be permeated with the presence of the triune God, then all of creation will be "happified" and all believers will be infinitely happy in the infinitely happy God. I close this excursus with a lengthy, but worthy quote by the puritan Stephen Charnock:

The happiness depends upon the presence of God, with whom believers shall be for ever present. Happiness cannot perish as long as God lives.... The enjoyment of God will be as fresh and glorious after many ages as it was at first. God is eternal, and eternity knows no change; there will then be the fullest possession, without any decay in the object enjoyed. There can be nothing past, nothing future; time neither adds to it, nor detracts from it; that infinite fulness of perfection which flourisheth in him now, will flourish eternally, without any discolouring of it in the least by those innumerable ages that shall run to eternity, much less any despoiling him of them.... He will have variety to increase delights, and eternity to perpetuate them; this will be the fruit of the enjoyment of an infinite, an eternal God. He is not a cistern, but a fountain, wherein water is always living, and never putrifies.[158]

Eden in Our Hearts

As the high priest would wear a memorial stone of Eden—somewhere he had never been—on his shoulders, so we long for what we have yet to experience. It is paradoxical in a sense to understand that we will one day fulfill a desire we have always had the appetite for, but never had the luxury to taste for ourselves.

The paradox lies in that we will taste life as it always was meant to be, but as we never previously had it. This is because we were designed to have a longing for the new world. Scripture is accurate at diagnosing our innate desire when it says that God has "put eternity in man's heart" (Ecclesiastes 3:11 ESV)

I once saw a video that went viral on Facebook; it had a montage of people of all ages who were deaf and, due to the advances in technology, were caught on camera experiencing sound for the first time. It was so emotional that I had chills watching it. The looks on their faces as they heard what their loved ones sounded like for the first time said it all.

But what they were experiencing, although new to them, wasn't foreign or far out; they were experiencing something human, something they were supposed to have experienced all along and never had the opportunity to experience till that moment—sound.

Similarly, dwelling in the new creation won't be like going off to some foreign land, in which the customs, language, or people make us feel like total outsiders who don't have a place there. It will instead feel like coming home after a long journey, through much lesser conditions, and experiencing all of the nostalgia of what makes home *home*. Your true home will welcome you as you walk in and experience what you have been missing all along.

WORKBOOK

Chapter 7 Questions

Main Truth: The chasm between the sacred and the secular will be abolished as God makes the new Jerusalem radiate with His unveiled presence, typified through the holy of holies in the Old Testament.

Question: Why will there be no temple in the new creation? Why will there no longer be the sun and the moon for light? Do you think these statements are literal, figurative, or both?

_____

_____

_____

_____

_____

_____

_____

_____

_____

_____

_____

Question: Describe the connection between holiness and happiness. How do we glorify God by being happy in Him?

_____

_____

_____

_____

_____

_____

_____

_____

_____

_____

Question: "All the nostalgia of what makes home _home_ will welcome you as you walk in and experience what you have missed." What makes home _home_ to you? How do you think these earthly impressions of home will translate to heavenly realities?

_____

_____

_____

_____

_____

_____

_____

_____

_____

_____

Action: Write out a list of words or short phrases to describe the new creation. Compare and contrast them to the creation we already know and experience.

Chapter Seven Notes

Jesus said:
[Command now]
Love one another AS I

have loved you.
(Then he does)

CHAPTER EIGHT

The World Created for the Son

The first Eden was made for Adam and his bride; the final Eden is going to be made for Christ and His bride.

Read: Revelation 22:1–5

After nearly a decade of preparations, in 2009, James Cameron released what was a cinematic masterpiece— *Avatar* (the movie with the blue people). What captured people's attention in that movie wasn't necessarily the script or the acting; it was the stunning beauty of Pandora.

I remember sitting in the theater enthralled, as my eyes saw what my mind had always pictured the world should look like. It was the lush vegetation, the vibrant colors like neon highlighters, the flowing streams of water and waterfalls, and the harmony in which the creatures dwelled among the creation. It all seemed like a dance, glorifying whomever would get the credit for creating such a place.

As the movie progressed, the plot and the characters

faded, and my mind ran wild, imagining what life might be like in Pandora. Over the years, I have not forgotten how I felt when I first saw that movie, and it has ignited my imagination even more ever since.

However, my imagination is not fixated on some far-off fantasy that will never come to fruition; on the contrary, my imagination is fixated on the promised new world that God will create and in which He will dwell fully, as promised throughout the Bible. Even the beauty of James Cameron's Pandora doesn't hold a candle to the awe of the new world promised in Scripture.

Paradoxically Nostalgic and New

And he showed me the river of the water of life, bright as crystal, flowing out from the throne of God and of the Lamb in the middle of the street of the city, and on both sides of the river is the tree of life, producing twelve fruits, yielding its fruit according to every month, and the leaves of the tree are for the healing of the nations.
—***Revelation 22:1–2*** *(my translation)*

John wants us to read Revelation 21–22 in the light of Genesis 1–2. We should feel a sense of biblical nostalgia. Genesis begins with the first Eden, and Revelation ends with the last Eden.

The nostalgia is paradoxical, because with as much as we feel a sense of longing for something from the far distant past, it is also something totally new. The continuity of the new creation will also contain discontinuity, which C.S. Lewis, eloquently, has helped us understand (see chapter 6).

And that is how Revelation often reads. It is like John struggles to find the right words to communicate what he is seeing, even under the influence of the Holy Spirit guiding his hand! To say that Eden has been restored is not to do justice to what the Scriptures say.

For example, the original Eden never had the throne of God and the Lamb. God ruled from heaven above, but now He dwells with His people on earth. Eden has been elevated and expanded for the glory of God and for the enjoyment of His people throughout all eternity.

The Life-Giving Garden

I have never met someone who was completely satisfied with the world the way it is. Even the most content of souls, if they are honest, will admit that our desires are weighty and that the lives we currently live cannot saturate them.

It is no accident that we feel the way we do. I have never met someone who would say this world matches up with all of their ideals. And if we are honest, this world is far worse than we even admit. Not only this world, but we, individually, are both the victims and the culprits of such depravity.

In high school, I was a wrestler. This required supreme conditioning and discipline. There were some practices when I would be so thirsty that nothing else was on my mind. Finishing the drill to obtain a drink of water was all that mattered. All of us have an unquenchable thirst for a drink of something we have never yet tasted.

In John 4, Jesus spoke to a woman at a well, in metaphorical language, about eternal life, alluding to it as "water." He then, in John 4:14, declared to this woman, "Whoever drinks of this water which I will give to him will never be thirsty for eternity, but the water which I will give to him will become in him a well of water springing up to eternal life."

What Jesus did was to contrast natural solutions for solving our deepest needs with supernatural solutions. Those who drank natural water would thirst again and would still eventually die. In stark contrast, those who drank of Jesus' "living water" would be satisfied and obtain eternal life.

The solution to all of our needs and desires is not within us, as much as pop culture promotes this to be the case. No, it is outside of us and inside the Lord Jesus—who invites us to drink of Him and find life. Only God can satisfy a person's deepest desire, because we are created in His image.

It is as John Flavel said: "[Christ] is bread to the hungry, water to the thirsty, a garment to the naked, healing to the wounded; and whatever a soul can desire is found in him."[159] Revelation 22:17 invites the "one who is thirsty" to drink the "water of life freely." This reminds us, yet again, that all of God's eschatological blessings are received by grace.

The first two verses of Revelation 22 reveal a life-giving garden that will undo the effects of sin in the present life. The same angel who showed John the vision of the New Jerusalem now shows him a vision of the new Eden—the place where our God-given thirst can be quenched.

There are two main elements in the Edenic garden that demand our attention: "the river of the water of life" and "the tree of life." Both are life-giving elements that are given by God and promote an environment of vibrant, unending existence.

The "river of the water of life" is nostalgic of the rivers in Eden and Ezekiel 47:1–12. At its core meaning, the river is a symbol of eternal life.[160] But within this broad meaning, we find more specific illustrations of its symbolism. Psalm 36 speaks of the loyal love of God and the blessing of knowing Him: "You feed them from the abundance of your own house, letting them drink from your river of delights. For you are the fountain of life, the light by which we see."[161]

The word translated here as "delights" is a fascinating word. In the Hebrew, it is the plural of the word "Eden," and certainly this psalm highlights the joy of the future by looking back at Eden before the Fall.[162] The psalm recognizes, as does the book of Revelation, that while Eden may have rivers of life, God is the fountain of life. For every abundant stream, God is the source. Jeremiah 2:13 even calls God the "fountain of living water."

While the river of Revelation 22 has rich symbolism, I do not believe this negates the idea that the new creation will have lush flowing rivers, perhaps even mystic both in appearance and effect.

The word for "bright" is the Greek word *lampros*,[163] which is the same word used to describe Jesus as the "bright morning star" (Revelation 22:16) and the angels as clothed in "bright linen" (Revelation 15:6). Jesus even said that the righteous would "shine like the sun in the king-dom" (Matthew 13:43).

Therefore, since we already saw that everything in the new creation, including the people inhabiting it, seems to radiate light and beauty, it would not be surprising to take the adjectival phrase, describing the river as "bright as crystal," to have an illuminating aspect.[164]

Karl Regstorf writes, "What [the book of Revelation] has to say about the river of the water of life shows that the end will not merely be a restoration of the beginning in Paradise, but will be something new in which God con-summates with unrestricted fullness the works and ways begun at creation."[165]

Perhaps Revelation provides the fulfilled meaning of Psalm 46: "There is a river whose streams gladden God's city, the holiest dwelling of the Most High."[166]

Hearing the words "bright as crystal" makes me think of bioluminescence, like the 'red tide' phenomenon, popu-lar on some coastlines—it is truly extraordinary. During the day it isn't anything appealing; however, when dusk breaks, the sea shore seems to light up in a luminescent blue color, like neon. It is surreal. This happens when phy-toplankton are disturbed in the water by movement, emitting a soft bluish glow due to a specific chemical reac-tion that takes place between the algae and surrounding oxygen. Unfortunately, this is actually something that kills many fish. I imagine something with even more grandeur than the 'red tide' phenomenon will make the rivers of the new world "bright as crystal," except it will be life-giving to the ecosystem instead of life-threatening. But even my best speculation is destined to fall short to the glory of the new creation.

The other important element we have in this garden-city is the tree of life, which may be foreign to many modern readers, but was very familiar to the ancient audience. In Jesus' letters to the churches, He motivates the believers with eschatological rewards that will be theirs to receive if they can endure in the faith.

While these rewards are for every believer, Jesus uses the context of the church to speak the language of the recipients in their best understanding. In the letter to the church in Ephesus (Revelation 2:1–7), Jesus promises that the one who prevails will be able to eat from the tree of life, something even Adam and Eve never got to do. This is the promise of immortality.

The Tree of Life

One of the recipients of the letter of Revelation, Ephesus was an important city in the early Church. John, who penned Revelation, knew the city of Ephesus and knew that they would understand the tree of life motif that he communicated to them in Revelation 2:7, specifically, and generally throughout the rest of the letter.

Ephesus was a vibrant city, beyond many others of its day. The city attracted worshipers from all around, stimulating the economy. But what had they come to worship? Along with other deities that were worshiped, Artemis (the goddess of fertility) had a special temple dedicated to her in Ephesus.[167]

Excavations and historical sources have given us keen insight into ancient Ephesus. It has become clear that the magnificent Temple of Artemis (one of the wonders of the ancient world) was accompanied by a robust garden. In the center of the garden was a tree shrine, most likely that of an oak or an elm tree.

The evidence leans to support that the "tree shrine" was the most sacred part of the temple and could very well have been spoken of as the "tree of life." Worship of Artemis was certainly the most popular of the Ephesian cults and was an important figure of civic pride.

To her was ascribed "unsurpassed cosmic power," including the power to raise people from the dead, according to Evans and Bubeck.[168] Why was this reward chosen for the Ephesians? Perhaps it is to contrast what paganism promised—access to the tree of life, which only Christianity could rightfully deliver.

Jewish apocalyptic literature was anything but silent about the expectancy of the tree of life reappearing in a radically renovated world. Consider three of these passages from outside biblical literature:

*Because it is for you that paradise is opened, **the tree of life** is planted, the age to come is prepared, plenty is provided, a city is built, rest is appointed, goodness is established and wisdom perfected beforehand. The root of evil is sealed up from you, illness is banished from you, and death is hidden; Hades has fled and corruption has been forgotten; sorrows have passed away, and in the end the treasure of immortality is made manifest.*
    —2 Esdras 8:52–54[169]

*And he shall open the gates of paradise, and shall remove the threatening sword against Adam. And he shall give to the saints to eat from **the tree of life**, and the spirit of holi*

ness shall be on them.
　　　　　—*Testament of Levi 18:10–11*[170]

And as for this sweet-smelling tree [the tree of life], no flesh has power to touch it until the great decision, in which there is vengeance for all and a completion forever. Then its fruit will be given to the just and holy chosen ones for life and for food; and it will be transplanted to the holy place from the house of God, King of the age.
　　　　　—*1 Enoch 25:4*[171]

Clearly, Jewish expectation reveals that the tree is a symbol of eschatological life and immortality given to the righteous.

The "tree of life" even finds its way into two more verses before the close of the letter—Revelation 22:14 and 18; verse 14 says, "Blessed are the ones who wash their robes, so that their authority will be over the tree of life and they may enter into the city through the gates."

Inheriting the tree of life is synonymous with inheriting immortality. Greater than the fountain of youth, the tree of life is an explicit symbol of the abolition of death, the curse of sin being lifted, and the anticipation of immortality realized by those who partake of its fruit.

Looking again at Revelation 22:1–2, we see that the tree of life is not only on one side, but both sides. It is possible that this is a grove of trees that give life. These trees produce "twelve fruits, yielding its fruit according to every month," indicating both the diverse variety and the accessible availability of the blessed fruit.

The ancient audience knew the reality of feast and famine. Human society was dependent on agriculture. Therefore, hearing about a tree giving fruit every month would be an immense encouragement, strengthening the idea that the new creation will be a place of abundance. Plus, if fruit and food can taste this good in a fallen world, I can only fathom how it will taste in a redeemed world!

And the leaves that provide "healing for the nations" embody the fulfillment of Ezekiel 47:12 almost verbatim. But what needs healing in a world with no death or sickness? This, I propose, is a healing from the emotional wounds of the present life. How wonderful it is to think that the emotional scars we have will find a bliss that can undo even the worst of our sufferings.

While the original Eden was "very good," the eschatological Eden is perfect, in every sense of the word. Beale writes, "Both Ezekiel 47 and Revelation 22:1–2 picture a recapitulation of the original garden of Eden, though in an even more escalated fertile form."[172] The flourishing conditions and lush nature make the first Eden dry in comparison.

Elements like the river of the water of life, bright as crystal, outdo the river of Eden. The tree of life on both sides, creating groves of trees, trumps the single tree of the first garden. This is a life-giving garden, whose symbolism is matched only by its vibrant, colorful elegance.

Other supplementary Old Testament passages help paint the picture for us. Joel 3:18 speaks of "mountains" that will "drip new wine." Amos says something similar and elaborates, "the hills will flow with" this sweet wine. This is a symbolic picture of feast and festivity, abundance and euphoria.

Not only will our needs be provided for, but luxurious blessings such as wine will be "flowing" in the mountain and the hills. Even animals will live in abundance and peace, without needing to eat each other or threaten the harmony of our existence by posing a danger to us. "They will not destroy" anyone or anything (cf. Isaiah 11:6–9). There will be plenty for all, and there will be harmony in all the new ecosystem.

The description of the new creation in Revelation 21:1– 22:5 suggests a unique blend of elements of architecture and nature. It is indeed a description of a 'garden-city.' Singapore is the closest thing; the whole city is an expanding garden. Giant man-made structures have been built with imports of nature. Trees, flowers, and other parts that form an ecosystem are cultivated on the outside and inside of many buildings. Thanks to this new ecosystem, there has been a return of some wildlife to the city, encouraging people everywhere that there is a possibility for mankind's habitation to blend well with animals of all sorts. The architects of the city have revealed that they truly believe mankind has an innate desire to live among nature.

Our advances in technology don't have to assume the depreciation of nature or threat its existence. Singapore is showing us not only what I see as a foreshadowing of the garden-city described, but a present reality where mankind can be good caretakers of the original creation, even before the arrival of the new creation. Whereas ecologists often fear the future of this earth, due to its inevitable decay, it is encouraging to know that someday God will make a glorious new earth on which the ecological problems that now plague our reality will no longer exist.

This does not imply that we should do nothing about present ecological problems; on the contrary we should work for solutions to these problems, and not with a feeling of despair, but in the confidence of God's promised coming new creation.

Looking into the Eyes of the Creator

And every curse will be no more, and the throne of God and of the Lamb will be in it, and His servants will serve Him, and they will see His face for themselves, and His name will be on their foreheads.

—Revelation 22:3-4 *(my translation)*

This verse encapsulates some of the most satisfying language in all of Scripture, when understood properly. Revelation 22:3 is reiterating that the garden of God will be life-giving and that all of creation will be void of "every curse."

Curse language is inextricably tied to the ramifications resulting from the Fall (cf. Genesis 3) and describes that which is unacceptable to God. The lifting of the curse means that the presence and the effects of sin will be no more! Death and decay are unacceptable to God and foreign to the life of heaven.

This fulfills the promise to the churches in Revelation 2:11, in which the prevailer is promised to "never be harmed by the second death." In Isaiah's last vision of the new creation, Isaiah 66:22–24, Isaiah prophesies about the everlasting life that is to be anticipated, lasting forever, "from new moon to new moon."

He concludes his vision with a graphic warning to its hearers, suggesting that the people of God will "go out and look at the corpses of the people who have rebelled against" God (Isaiah 66:24a).

The first death was destructive, but God's mercy allowed redemption through Christ. The second death is permanent. Those who face the second death will not be given life again; they are destroyed, never able to destroy God's good creation again. Anthony Hoekema eloquently notes:

> The total work of Christ is nothing less than to redeem this entire creation from the effects of sin. That purpose will not be accomplished until God has ushered in the new earth, until Paradise Lost has become Paradise Regained. We need a clear understanding of the doctrine of the new earth, therefore, in order to see God's redemptive program in cosmic dimensions. We need to realize that God will not be satisfied until the entire universe has been purged of all the results of man's fall.[173]

Since God's dwelling, heaven itself, has now made its home on the new earth, "the throne of God and of the Lamb" is appropriately there in the garden city. The Greek verb *latreuo*, translated here as "serve," carries the idea of service through worship and worship through service. It denotes the meaning "to serve as priest."[174] Serving God in this priestly sense has more of the connotation of worshipful relationship. Basically, in response to God creating us for Himself, revealing Himself to us, and being steadfast in His love towards us—we respond with adoration and worship, declaring God as the supreme object of our affection. This is what it means to serve God—to adore Him and do all things in response to what He has first done for us.

The ministry of this worshipful service is exclusively offered to God in both the Old and New Testaments (unless pagans were worshiping false gods).[175] According to this verse, believers will, as a kingdom of priests (cf. 1 Peter 2:9), serve and worship "Him." To whom is the "Him" referring? God? Or the Lamb? The answer is yes. Both.[176]

The singular "Him" indicates the unity of the Father and the Son in receiving worship, which is not surprising considering the numerous instances for unity throughout Revelation between the two distinct persons of the single divine essence.[177] Observe this helpful correlation chart I title "Like Father, Like Son":

The Father	The Son
Hair like white wool (Daniel 7:9, speaking of the Ancient of Days)	Hair like white wool (Revelation 1:14)
King of kings and Lord of lords (1 Timothy 6:15; cf. Deuteronomy 10:17)	King of kings and Lord of lords (Revelation 17:14; 19:16; cf. Acts 17:17)
*The First and the Last (Isaiah 41:4; 44:6; 48:12, Note that it is Yahweh, the Lord, speaking in these)	The First and the Last (Revelation 1:17; 2:8)
The Alpha and Omega (Revelation 21:6)	The Alpha and Omega (Revelation 22:13; Revelation 1:8)
Worshiped as deity (Revelation 4:8–11)	Worshiped as deity (Revelation 5:8–12)
Worshiped with [Jesus] the Lamb (Revelation 5:13–14)	Worshiped with the one on the throne [the Father] (Revelation 5:13–14)
Conclusion: The Father shares in the same essence of deity as the Son while being distinct in person and role. Both are co-equal and co-eternal.	Conclusion: The Son shares in the same essence of deity as the Father while being distinct in person and role. Both are co-equal and co-eternal.

We now arrive at possibly the most glorious phrase in all of Revelation: "And they will see His face for themselves, and His name will be on their foreheads" (Revelation 22:4, my translation). To truly understand the magnitude of this passage, we have to unpack a few truths of biblical theology.

Back in Exodus 33:18–23, we find Moses pleading with God to show him His glory (Exodus 33:18). God responds to Moses with this:

> And he said, "I myself will cause all my goodness to pass over before you, and I will proclaim the name of Yahweh before you, and I will be gracious to whom I will be gracious, and I will show compassion to whom I will show compassion." But he said, "You are not able to see my face, because a human will not see me and live." And Yahweh said, "There is a place with me, and you will stand on the rock. And when my glory passes over, I will put you in the rock's crevice, and I will cover you with my hand until I pass over. And I will remove my hand, and you will see my back, but my face will not be visible."
>
> —*Exodus 33:19–23*

First off, whoa! Second, we can learn here something significant about God's nature—God's face cannot be seen by fallen creatures, not even biblical heroes like Moses.[178] However, ever since ancient times, this has been what human beings have longed for, to see their Maker—the One whose image we are hand-crafted in the likeness of.

This stems from the ancient belief that to see God's face means to know Him as He actually is. Richard Bauckham comments, "The face expresses who a person is. To see God's face will be to know who God is in his personal being. This will be the heart of humanity's eternal joy in their eternal worship of God."[179]

It was considered the pinnacle of blessing to have God's face shine upon you (cf. Numbers 6:25).[180] And so it became part of Jewish liturgy to exhort one another to seek the face of God (e.g., Psalm 24:6; 27:8; 105:4), which would seem like a journey full of dejection if there was no hope of the new creation.

Eschatology developed as the canon of Scripture did, and it became clear that seeing the face of God would be the highest hope of the righteous and the means of their greatest satisfaction. "Because I am righteous, I will see you. When I awake, I will see you face to face and be satisfied" (Psalm 17:15 NLT).[181] Jesus affirmed this expectation in Matthew 5:8 when He said that the "poor in spirit" are "blessed" because "they will see God."

Revelation 21–22 has been a constant unraveling of language that presents the fact that God's presence is more intimate than we could have imagined. It starts off broad, but beautiful, with God making His home with us (Revelation 21:1–8).

Then we discover that the heavenly city will be a cosmic holy of holies (Revelation 21:9–27), where God's presence was a privilege exclusively experienced by the high priest. Finally, there is the highest form of divine intimacy granted to us, as God doesn't stop at making His home with us or gracing us with His presence, but actually shows us His face (Revelation 22:4), something never afforded to any human before.

"They will see His face for themselves" (Revelation 22:4).[182] But whose face, exactly, shall we see? God the

Father? God the Son? Again, as was the case in verse 3, the answer is yes. Both.[183] To stare upon the Creator of the cosmos and gaze upon His beauty is a privilege we are wildly underestimating.

This is *the* face of God we are talking about here. For all the magnificent, breathtaking, out-of-this-world wonders in the universe that we can see with modern technology,[184] none can surpass what the face of God must look like.

Scripture tells us, "Whenever he is revealed we will be like him, because we will see him just as he is" (1 John 3:2). This encourages us that being face to face with God (as 1 Corinthians 13:12 anticipates) will be such a transformative experience for us, that suddenly our sanctification will be complete, for "we will be like him."[185]

How can this be? How can seeing someone, even God, change us so radically? I know this can be true, even from an experience I have had on this side of life. As a husband, I remember as my bride, Ariana, walked down the aisle. She was the most beautiful bride imaginable, and to my eyes, it was as if no one else was present in the room. In that moment, nothing else and no one else could have lured me away from her. The temptation of adultery was not only not an option, but not even a thought—because she had my undivided desire.

One day, we will gaze upon the source and quintessence of beauty, and nothing else will ever take our gaze off of Him in loyal love. This is to be the climax of our happiness; the satisfaction of our souls; the heaven of heaven—to see the face of God. We will see the face of the Creator of the cosmos and our whole life's pains will melt away as our hearts burn with passionate love.

Some have asked, "How do we know that we will not sin in heaven?" We know this because there will be nothing, absolutely nothing, that is able to pull us away from the unveiled beauty of God. As the first sin was rooted in thinking there was another way, there won't be any ounce of temptation. The life we will have will not even allow us to wonder about something better.

Spurgeon says, "They 'shall see his face;' by which I understand two things: first, that they shall literally and physically, with their risen bodies, actually look into the face of Jesus; and secondly, that spiritually their mental faculties shall be enlarged, so that they shall be enabled to look into the very heart, and soul, and character of Christ, so as to understand him, his work, his love, his all in all, as they never understood him before."[186]

My understanding is that the new, resurrected, imperishable bodies we will be given will be powerful enough and able to live to behold the face of God in its full glory, as we will be glorified by His glory and for His glory.

Spurgeon continues, "And this involves a fifth privilege, namely, *complete transformation.* 'They shall be like him, for they shall see him as he is.' If they see his face they shall be 'changed from glory to glory' by this face-to-face vision of the Lord. Beholding Christ, his likeness is photographed upon them; they become in all respects like him as they gaze upon him [in a] world without end."[187]

Previously, I noted that to see God's face implies knowing Him personally with an extensively intimate knowledge. This is important. Knowledge is the basis of love. It is the foundation to loving God. How are we ever going to love a God whom we don't know? Men, ask yourselves, how important is knowing your wife in being able to effectively love her? You can only love your wife to the extent that you know her! Women, you are not excluded from this, know your man, and love him well.

The face-to-face relationship we will have with God is followed up by one more detail: "His name will be on their foreheads." The name of God on the forehead is ultimately a sign of protection, belonging, and closeness of relationship.

In the Old Testament, the high priest wore the sacred name of God on his forehead and entered the holy of holies, where God's immediate presence presided. The golden plate on the forehead would be engraved with the words: "Holy to Yahweh."[188] This allusion intensifies the notion that all believers will have the priestly privilege of intimate nearness to God.

In the book of Revelation, the name on the forehead tells of one's allegiance and belonging. There are only two options: one is either marked by God or by the beast.[189] Those marked on their forehead by God are sealed and protected from God's impending wrath (cf. Revelation 7:3; 9:4).

The name on the forehead fulfills the promise to the prevailer, back in Revelation 3:12. Jesus Himself said that He would "write on him the name of my God and the name of the city of my God, the new Jerusalem that comes down from heaven from my God, and my new name." The name of God being written on the Christian highlights the believer's being God's beloved possession, belonging only to Him, marked out by Him to receive His love and affection.

Osborne provides a helpful insight: "Not only will they have a permanent home but also a new name written on them.... It is 'the name of my God,' fitting the adoption imagery of Romans 8:15 (by the Spirit we cry 'Abba Father!') and signifying that we partake of his essence as his children. There is also probably an echo of Isaiah 62:2, the 'new name bestowed' by Yahweh on faithful Israel."[190]

The name of the city being written on the Christian symbolizes authentic citizenship in the coming heavenly city. They will be the rightful owners of this city. Like a parking space marked off exclusively for an important person, the New Jerusalem is a city to be exclusively enjoyed by those who are marked by God and have the name of the city written on them.

Lastly, the writing of Christ's "new name" is a little ambiguous, but it certainly indicates a special relationship. Because biblical imagery continuously points to the believer's union with Christ being the true form of marriage, I think Christ writing His name on us is previewed by how, in modern American culture, the woman being wed takes on the man's last name, and thus inherits all that he has and all that he is.

In a similar fashion, Christ wishes to love His bride with all that He is and to give her all that He has. And because Christ has a "name above every name" (Philippians 2:9), we can trust that there is nothing outside of His royal rule that would ever threaten us.

The Kingdom of the Son

*And night will be no more, and they will have no need of the
light of a lamp and the light of the sun, because the Lord
God will shine on them, and they will reign forever into
eternity.*

—**Revelation 22:5** *(my translation)*

The reign of the triune God is not something we pas-
sively will observe. Astonishingly, God will entrust His
redeemed people to reign with Him. In the ultimate turn of
events, the believer, once a condemned sinner, becomes,
by God's transformational love, a crowned saint reigning
with Christ the King. There is no place for human hierar-
chy in this because the Lord will be King and we will be
individually equal, participating in the collective whole as
we live out the adventurous responsibility of being kings
with the King over the new creation.

Commentator Richard Brooks celebrates: "We shall
share in Christ's royalty and we shall live like kings. And
we shall be like this for ever and ever!"[191] While Revelation 22:3 shows us as priests participating in worshipful
service, Revelation 22:5 shows us as kings reigning over
the new creation. Daniel 7:18 prophesied of the day when
God's people would "receive the kingdom" and possess it
"forever and ever," something that comes to fruition in this
passage.

The crowns we are given upon passing into glory (Revelation 2:10; 3:11) will be put to use as we are given royal
responsibilities, as part of the family of God forever. What
was sung about in hopeful expectation (Revelation 5:10)

will now be a cosmic reality.

This seems to restore the image of God in which mankind was originally created in (Genesis 1:26–27) to its highest glory, even beyond that of Adam. Part of imaging God is living with a sense of resolve. And as we fulfill our purpose, we feel satisfaction.

This design in us won't end upon our death. In the new world, we will certainly still live with intention and take immense delight in being purposeful as we reign with Christ. "Boring" will be a word of the past, void of any present meaning, banished from our vocabulary as we carry out our calling as kingdom royalty ruling with King Jesus. What will be our royal responsibilities? I don't know. But I do know that the innate desire in each of us to live a life of significance will be infinitely satisfied as we live eternal lives that are exhilarating and full of purpose.

As a wedding is a celebration of a new beginning, so the end of history is the new beginning of life itself. Everything will be new. Everything that has been redeemed will reach its highest form of potential and purpose. And there is a purpose and recipient who receives the new world. It will be as Jonathan Edwards writes: "The end of God's creating the world, was to prepare a kingdom for his Son, (for he is appointed heir of the world,) which should remain to all eternity."[192]

An excerpt from the Dead Sea Scrolls' discovery from the ancient world (4Q475 5–6) not only affirms that the new earth will become like Eden, but that it will be ruled by a son; it says, "All the world will be like Eden, and all...the earth will be at peace forever, and...a beloved son...will...inherit it all."[193] It has been destined since before the first creation that the Son of God would be the rightful owner of the new creation.

This is what Scripture alludes to in Colossians 1:13, when believers are said to be "transferred" to the "kingdom of the Son." In the same vein, Hebrews 1:8 says that God the Father applies Psalm 45:6 to the Son, saying, "Your throne, O God, is forever and ever, and the scepter of righteous is the scepter of your kingdom." Surely it is a joint "kingdom of Christ and God" (Ephesians 5:5; cf. Revelation 11:15).

But perhaps the primary reason Jesus is revealed to mankind as the "Son of God" is to tell about His functional role as heaven's Prince, who came down to redeem the world and become King of all the new creation.[194]

But what king reigns without his bride? The King of kings has chosen His bride and marks her with His name (Revelation 3:12; 22:4); He then rules with her forever (Revelation 22:5). We have alluded to the marital language in Revelation throughout this book. This language takes us back to the Old Testament, in which the Lord claims to be a spouse to His people.

This is a constant motif throughout the Bible. Isaiah 54:5 makes a strong appeal that the Lord ("your Maker") is the spouse of His people. It is difficult to miss this theme, but it is also challenging to deal with such a robust reality in a concise manner. Perhaps one of the most eloquent verses that sums up this theme from the Old Testament is Hosea 2:19–20, which reads:

And I [the Lord] will betroth you to me forever. I will betroth you to me in righteousness and in justice, in steadfast

love and in mercy. I will betroth you to me in faithfulness.
And you shall know the Lord.

—**Hosea 2:19–20** *(ESV)*

The New Testament picks up this theme and adds something provocative. In Ephesians 5:32, Paul says this: "This mystery is great, but I am speaking with reference to Christ and the church." He calls human marriage, which is the first marriage, a signpost pointing to the final marriage between Christ and the Church.

All other metaphors in the Bible are using the substance to relate to the shadow. For example, Christ and the Church are like vines and branches (cf. John 15), using an already existing and natural element for analogous purposes. But none are like the metaphor of marriage, in which the man and the woman are the prototype and the metaphor but not the final form of marriage. Christ and the Church are the reality. Men and women are the shadow, but Christ and the Church are the substance of marriage.

The first Eden was made for Adam and his bride; the final Eden will be made for Christ and His Bride.[195] The puritan Thomas Goodwin concurs: "As Adam had a world made for him, so shall Jesus Christ, this second Adam—Adam being a type of him that was to come—have a world made for him. This world was not good enough for him; he hath a better appointed than that which old Adam had, a new heaven and a new earth, according to the promise, Isaiah 66:22, where the saints shall reign."[196]

Jesus Is So Much More

There is a Christian phrase, a cliché, that I would like to spend a moment debunking. Perhaps you have heard it; it goes something like this: "If we were perfect, we wouldn't need Jesus." Oh, how many times I have cringed when I have heard pastors or laypersons state this phrase.

Adhering to this phrase would admit that if we were perfect, we would not have a relationship with Christ. And before going any further, I have to challenge this phrase in its definition of "perfect." If perfection is determined by moral finality and ethical purity, then we are working with an incomplete definition.

As I mentioned back in chapter 1, "sinless" is not the equivalent of "perfection." Otherwise, Adam and Eve would have lived in perfection, and we saw how that turned out. It is worth reiterating that Adam and Eve did not experience the highest form of life. Yes, it was far superior to what we are currently experiencing, but it was also far inferior to the life that we will experience after the eschaton.

The aforementioned phrase implies that Christianity should be twisted into what we can gain from our Savior, like a leech sucking the life out of its host. We do not come to our Lord like we would a drinking fountain, to gain sustenance, only to depart until we need our thirst quenched again. Is Jesus only the pardon for our sins? If so, then most of the American church is giving adequate time to Him by paying homage to Him only a few Sundays out of the month.

However, if Jesus is much more than the paschal lamb

who takes away our sins (and He is), then how can we not give our utmost devotion to Him? How can we not adore Him? Wouldn't our cherishing of Jesus lead us to even more joy? And wouldn't the possession of more joy in Him lead us to cherish Him even more?

We must abandon the thought that dependency is something we are to outgrow when it comes to our relationship with the triune God. Our modern culture is obsessed with independence. Even our moral compass has trekked a new course, further and further away from the heart and holiness of God.

But as Christians, we are admittedly and unashamedly dependent. The moment we sincerely and wholeheartedly put our faith in Jesus, we begin a new life. Being rescued from the depths of sin and its consequences, we embark on a voyage intrinsically connected to the life of our Savior.

Those who want the pleasures that come from God, apart from the person of God, will find that they have neither. You can only have the pleasures of God through and with the person of God. Our Hero didn't wish to rescue us to see us fall for another, He wishes to take the harlot He has redeemed to be His bride and bless her with all that He has and all that He is. Our dependency upon Christ is as the oneness of male and female becoming one flesh through the bond of marriage.

I propose we forgo the previous phrase and have our souls meditate on a new one: *Salvation commences when Jesus satisfies our supreme need; salvation culminates when Jesus satisfies our infinite desire.*

When examining this phrase that has become a recurring meditation of mine, we see that our Savior is not only the source or vehicle toward eternal life—He is the goal of it all. Relationship with Jesus, classically called "union with Christ," *is* the heaven of heaven.

Of all the thrills I believe we are to experience in the new creation, I am confident none can eclipse the reciprocal love and happiness to be found in Him. To "see His face," as Revelation 22:4 says, is to see His unveiled glory. The beauty that would blind us in our current physical bodies will be visible in our resurrection bodies. We will behold the King in His beauty, as Isaiah prophesied.[197]

Our salvation begins with the realization of our pressing need for Jesus. Then, as we serve and fellowship with our Lord Jesus over the years, He becomes so much more to us than a "need." One day we will say, "At first I needed You, but now I desire You. I have no love for anyone or anything the way I have for You. All I am is yours."

Then, the King of heaven will look into our eyes and say, "I spoke vows to you before you were born. All *I am* is yours. I sang those words to you before I made you. I loved you in eternity past. My love has had no beginning and it will have no end. Enter into My happiness. Be engulfed in the euphoria of My majestic presence. Dive to the depths and ascend to the heights of My love. Cherish that your spirit is now and forevermore interwoven with Mine. Be made new. Be My bride. Reign with Me. Forever and always."

And so it is revealed that redemption is the greatest story of divine romance. As the life of the new world is one in which the foreshadowing of the first creation comes to fruition in the new. The world of heaven is wed with our world. The King of heaven marries us. And we will reign in a world without end. And we can rest in these words: "Those who are married to Jesus," Spurgeon says, "will be endlessly happy."[198]

In preparation for such a wonderful experience, we cannot exhaust our imagination to the point that our highest hopes are not met with the utmost satisfaction. We can imagine, even dream, with words that take any human language to the border of its ability and still fail to grasp the heights of such an experience.

To see the face of God will be the heaven of heaven. We will truly discover, if we are not convinced already, that Jesus not only has satisfied our greatest need, but that He will forever and ever satisfy us. We will continue to indulge in that satisfaction in the new creation, where time is irrelevant and bliss is boundless. Endless adventure awaits us, and I express my excitement by inviting anyone and everyone to know the God who is the author of such everlasting delight.

WORKBOOK

Chapter Eight Questions

Main Truth: While the first Eden presented life as "very good," the final Eden will be truly perfect in every sense of the word. We will live in the temple/garden-city serving the Lord and reigning with Him in intimate fellowship.

Question: Have you ever met someone in person after building a friendship online first? What was the experience like? What did you learn from being "face to face" that you could not learn any other way? How will our relationship with God change when we finally behold His face?

_____

_____

_____

_____

_____

_____

_____

_____

_____

_____

_____

Question: How is marriage a picture of the new creation?
What attributes of marriage will characterize our experience as the Bride of Christ?

_____

_____

_____

_____

_____

_____

_____

_____

_____

_____

Question: What does the phrase "Jesus is so much more"
mean to you? How can we cherish Him as our Savior

while also appreciating Him as far more than just a ticket to heaven?

_____

_____

_____

_____

_____

_____

_____

_____

_____

_____

Action: Allow yourself to imagine the new creation. If you are artistic, draw out some of your ideas. If there is a song that you love about heaven, listen intently to it. If you journal, freely write out some of your imaginings and longings. Then meditate on this question: With such an eternity waiting for us, how should we live until we get there?

Chapter Eight Notes

CONCLUSION

The End Is the New Beginning

The life of a Christian is wondrously ruled in this world by the consideration and meditation of the life of another world.[199]

—**Richard Sibbes**

Read: Romans 8:18

The last book in C.S. Lewis's Chronicles of Narnia series, *The Last Battle,* has an immense focus on death. It is almost as if Lewis wanted to encourage the reader to rethink death and take a biblical perspective of it.

There is one scene, in particular, that I would like to bring to your attention. Aslan talks to the children, who have been with him throughout the stories, and who have experienced death without even really realizing it at this point in the story. Aslan says to them:

"There was a real railway accident," said Aslan softly. "Your father and mother and all of you are—as you used to call it in the Shadowlands—dead. The term is over: the holidays have begun. The dream is ended: this is morning."

And as He spoke He no longer looked to them like a lion; but the things that began to happen after that were so great and beautiful that I cannot write them. And for us this is the end of all the stories, and we can most truly say that they all lived happily ever after. But for them it was only the beginning of the real story. All their life in this world and all their adventures in Narnia had only been the cover and the title page: now at last they were beginning Chapter One of the Great Story which no one on earth has read: which goes on forever: in which every chapter is better than the one before.[200]

Welcome to Chapter One

C.S. Lewis was an absolute genius in how he wrote the conclusion to his Chronicles of Narnia. The paragraph I quoted above is one of the most influential to me in thinking through the purpose of how to conclude *this* book. We should see how the book of Revelation ties together all loose ends in the biblical story, but also how it shows us a picture of a new life—starting Chapter One of God's eternal destiny for us.

Genesis (the book of the beginning) and Revelation (the book of the end) bear such remarkable language that it is only appropriate to show how new creation concludes a perfect end to the Bible's message to us.

Genesis shows the original creation of the heavens and the earth (Genesis 1:1), and Revelation the new creation of the heavens and the earth (Revelation 21:1). Genesis contains the creation of the sun, the establishment of night, and the laying out of the sea (Revelation 1:16, 5, 10); Revelation describes the absence of these things in what they symbolized (Revelation 21:23; 22:5; 21:1).

Genesis contains the presence of the serpent (3:1); Revelation, the defeat of the dragon (20:10). Genesis morbidly reveals the entrance of the curse into the world and the penalty of death (3:14–17, 19); Revelation announces the reversal of the curse and the death of death (22:3; 21:4). Genesis expels sinners from Eden (3:24); Revelation invites the saints into an eternal, escalated Eden (22:14).

All of this preaches that Revelation, while certainly being about the end of human history as we know it, is more focused on the dawning of God's eternal reign over the cosmos as He ushers in the highest form of life for His redeemed people. Revelation is the drama and narrative of how the new creation will come about through King Jesus.

We must not—we cannot—think of the eternal state as the entrance into boredom. The arrival of the new creation is Chapter One of an unending adventure story, in which God's people live out a life far beyond what they could ever have imagined and far better than what they could have ever desired in this current age.

When speaking with engaged couples, it is typical to hear something like this: "I can't even think of anything past my wedding day." In some cases, they are expressing the sheer excitement they have for that day. For others, the stress of wedding planning can be something they can't wait to put behind them.

Either way, many couples seem to have tunnel vision and are fixated on the wedding day itself. There isn't anything inherently wrong with that. However, it is helpful for engaged couples to go through premarital counseling so that they are thinking of the days *beyond* the wedding as well.

Revelation 21 and 22 have provided us with just that perspective. After Jesus comes and administers the final judgment, all redeemed believers receive an apocalyptic, symbol-laden picture of life beyond the last day (the eschaton). For Christians, the end is the new beginning—Chapter One, if you will. We must keep that in mind as we think about life, death, afterlife, and the eternal state.

I specify the distinction between "afterlife" and the "eternal state" as a reminder that, if a Christian were to die and go to be with the Lord right now, that person still wouldn't be in the new creation—not yet. That person would be in bliss with God and other believers, but "heaven" as it is right now is not the eschaton. The consummation of the new creation hasn't happened yet, and thus every believer, even when that individual dies, is still joyfully waiting for that epic event.

My Imagination Ceased

As I write this, I am sitting at the cliffs of the central coast in California. This part of the country is a popular retirement spot due to its mild climate and breathtaking views. Taking it all in there provokes a paradoxical feeling welling up inside me.

Simultaneously, I am both content and complacent, satisfied but wanting much more than any experience on this side of life can offer. As silly as it may sound, I would like to jump from this coastal-cliff edge and soar among the birds, then dive deep into the ocean blue.

Why is it that even in some great moments—even in the best moments of our lives—there is a sense that nothing in this world can ever satisfy the longings of our innermost being? Is this why we are so captivated by movies or television series? For a few short and fleeting hours, we can allow our imaginations to run wild as we live vicariously through fictional or nonfictional characters.

One day, we will not need epic cinematography to entertain us. We will not need movie theaters to captivate our imaginations. Throughout this book, I have argued and implied that the greatest fantasy will one day become a reality for the believer in Christ. One day, our longings and imaginings for something more will cease.

How astounding is that? Right now, we have the capacity to imagine something better, something more— that's how our imagination enhances our lives. But when the consummation of all of God's promises happens, we will no longer be able to even imagine something better, because we will be living in the best of our best imagination's longings.

One day, at the eschaton, our imaginations will cease, and we will have every inkling of our desires satisfied— and it will never end. I celebrate the words of J.I. Packer when he says, "Hearts on earth say in the course of a joyful experience, 'I don't want this ever to end.' But it invariably does. The hearts of those in heaven say, 'I want this to go on forever.' And it will. There is no better news than this."[201]

I am so thankful for the information we do have on the subject of the coming new world, but I am also aware that the Bible doesn't answer every question we have, just some of the most important ones.[202] We are not given a map or an itinerary of our eternal home. Yet, Scripture is sufficient. And it has been a pleasure to examine the words of Scripture to find encouragement in what it says.

In the meantime, until all believers get to watch God finally usher in the new heavens and the new earth, we must wait with exuberant trust. We give our trust over to God, knowing that His idea for "heaven" is so much better than anything we could ever think of. We must also marvel at the mystery with trust, again.

I don't understand what our marriage union with Jesus will look like. I can't fathom how He will be able to love us all so collectively, yet so individually—so equally, yet so intimately. It is one of those things in which we must have a very rational faith that an infinite God will be able to blow away our finite expectations.

> I know not, oh, I know not, what joys are waiting there, what radiancy of glory, what bliss beyond compare![203]
> **—Richard Brooks**

I am echoing the prayer of the puritan Samuel Rutherford: "My desire is that my Lord would give me broader and deeper thoughts, to feed myself with wondering at His love."

Wonder is a healthy component of the Christian life that is far too often misplaced or misunderstood. The more we can get lost in the wonder of an infinite God, the more likely we will be effective in beautifying the world around us, specifically through the expansion of the gospel. "For I consider" the apostle Paul wrote, "that the sufferings of the present time are not worthy to be compared with the glory that is about to be revealed to us" (Romans 8:18).

Staying Present

Salvation is a present reality, not just a future hope. This book has stressed the latter. However, like reverse engineering, our knowledge of the future provides invaluable insights into the present. We can be truly present today because we don't have to worry about tomorrow.

We know the future is bright, so we can take on today. We can embrace the journey of this world, its trials included, because we know that dusk only lasts so long until the day breaks and the dawn of the new creation is here.

Second Corinthians 5:17 exhorts us, "Therefore if anyone is in Christ, he is a new creation; the old things have passed away; behold, new things have come." If you are a Christian, these words are for you—you are a new creation! Remember the word *kainos* from chapter 5? Well, that is the same word used here to explain the new nature of the Christian. This doesn't mean you have necessarily arrived, but it does mean that the resurrection glory and reigning power of Christ have been inaugurated in and through the life of Christians now.

Yes, there is *so* much more to look forward to, but that never, ever should negate our purposeful presence in the world today. You are a new creation. David Garland comments, "Paul's assumption is that being in Christ should bring about a radical change in a person's life."[204]

The context of 2 Corinthians 5 shows us that the blessing of being a new creation demands the duty to be "ambassadors" to the world and for the world. Garland continues, "Christians see the world in a new way and become new when they are joined to Christ."[205] This "new way" revolutionizes how we live now in light of our eternal hope.

The belief in eternal life gives meaning to everything we do. This means that today matters. We are to live compelling lives, determined to share the same gospel that dances in our hearts daily. Everything matters—every word, every action, and every day.

There is a poetic phrase, written by C.T. Studd, that has stuck with me ever since the first time I heard it: "Only one life, t'will soon be past, only what's done for Christ will last." When we weigh the cost of what we say "yes" or "no" to, we should think through this phrase. How are we using the time we have been given? Do we even consider the fate of those who don't know Jesus?

Paul's life motto in Philippians 1:21 should be our motto, too" "For to me to live is Christ and to die is gain." Think about how radical those words are and how compelling are the lives of those who live by them.

The truth is, death can only be a gain if the life to come is better than our existence now. But most people view the Christian afterlife as a boring and dull existence. We need to adopt Lewis's view of death and the language he uses in *The Last Battle*.

The world needs to see that living a life that is fixated on King Jesus is worthwhile, and that death is only our personal gain. Christians who have a healthy view of eschatology are paradoxically fearless of dying, but determined about living. These are the most effective Christians.

One day, I was taking a stroll in a gorgeous forest in the state of Washington. I noticed that I was missing many of the views because my head was slanted diagonally downward. My eyes were seeing dirt, footprints, and leftover gum from previous people.

It is not that the ground is always "ugly," but the best sights are usually around us and ahead of us. The forest trees, lush vegetation, and mountain horizons are what I should be looking at as I walk, so I started keeping my chin up and my eyes forward as I walk, whether I am now in a forest, at the beach, or just walking in the city.

With many Christians, I have noticed they do something similar in their spiritual lives. They are completely unaware of how the Bible gives us a lens to see the beauty of the Gospel around us in the present day, and how the beauty of the Gospel is ahead of us in the future.

That is the goal of this book. Instead of new creation being a lens that pulls us away from true reality, it pulls back the veil and shows us how God's salvation is the *true* reality. The greatest eternal hope imaginable (and beyond) is offered to those in Christ Jesus.

I want Christians to be able to live in the present and anticipate the future, embracing the paradoxical tension so much so that their lives reflect people entranced by the invasion of God's new life, even in the present life in this world.

The beauty of the Gospel in the present and the promised future should be as a walk in the woods, where we keep our heads up to see the beauty around us and the horizon in front of us toward which we are walking. So, Christian, keep your chin up! Both literally and metaphorically!

Teaching the World to Sing

The Indri lemurs of the jungles of Madagascar are fascinating creatures. They practice a morning ritual in which they congregate together, climb toward the tops of the trees, and sing. Some suggest this is their way of reminding themselves to celebrate that the jungle is their home. It is contagious.

I wonder what would happen if Christians took some inspiration from these lemurs. I am not suggesting we move to the jungle and sing "Kumbaya" together (although my wife wouldn't be opposed to doing just that!). Rather, what if the outside world looking in at the lives of Christians saw a community of people who lived beautifully and celebrated what God's salvific work does to creation?

Too many Christians treat this world as a piece of trash that God needs to crumple up and throw away. This pessimism doesn't do any favors to anyone, especially when it isn't grounded in realism. Because, as we have seen in this book, God has a plan of salvation for the cosmos. This isn't just me being optimistic; it is biblical.

Although this world and the inhabitants in it are deeply flawed, God is redeeming this world and those who wish to submit to His royal rule and receive His infinite love.

Maybe the lemurs are just trying to teach the world to sing. Perhaps Christians, in their gatherings, should also be less focused on leaving this world and being taken up to heaven and more concerned about cultivating this world and proactively anticipating the coming of heaven to earth. The best way to convert pagans is to show them the beauty of the Christ of Christianity.

Proverbs 4:18 says, "...the path of the righteous ones is like the light of dawn, leading and shining until the day is full". With God's saving work being inaugurated in the world through the Church, are we demonstrating the dawn of the new creation through the way we lead our lives?

Is the light that radiates from our lives a living metaphor that God's promised future is a bright one? Inspired by the lemurs, maybe we can stop buying in to the fear of the end and start teaching the world that we can sing with jubilant joy because God has not abandoned our universe.

Commenting on Proverbs 4:18, Raymond Ortlund Jr. notes, "...if you have chosen Christ, he is dawning in your life. There might be only a glimmer of light on your horizon right now. But the sun is rising, the darkness cannot stop it, and Christ will bring his good work in you to noonday brilliance.... That bright gospel confidence is how you keep going, step by step, moment by moment, on the right path."[206]

I wish to provide one final quote from Charles Spurgeon:

See the happiness which is promised us! Behold the heaven which awaits us! Forget for awhile your present cares: let all your difficulties and your sorrows vanish for a season; and live for awhile in the future which is so certified by faithful promises that you may rejoice in it even now! The veil which parts us from our great reward is very thin: hope gazes through its gauzy fabric. Faith, with eagle eyes, penetrates the mist which hides eternal delights from longing eyes.[207]

Christianity is best understood in the present in light of the future; and the future, in light of the present. By studying and meditating on the biblical lens of new creation, we give ourselves the chance to be able to offer people a hope beyond their wildest dreams, and more satisfying than anything we have ever settled for in this life.

I Invite you to join me in a lifestyle of deeply contemplating the wonder of the new world. In doing so, I believe you and I will be compelled to make the most of our present lives.

For those of you who are brothers and sisters in Christ, I say to you—I cannot wait to meet you, and share in the infinite joy ahead of us. To those who may not be a believer in Jesus, I plead with you at the conclusion of this book: give your life to Jesus. Trust in Him. I don't want you to miss the joy of knowing Him even now—but especially in the life to come.

Death does not prevent us from our destiny; it only propels us into Chapter One of our eternal destiny, as we go to be with the Lord and await the arrival of the new creation that will be ushered in at the return of Christ the King.

REFERENCES

Notes

1. Revelation chapters 6–20 tend to be highly controversial and debated. Chapter 20 specifically is the most debated section of Revelation. This book does not want to engage those chapters. While we may allude to something in them, we do not want to lose focus. There are great resources accessible in the discussion of Revelation 6–20, but that is another book for another day.

2. "Heaven" is in a quotation during this introduction, due to the fact that the way many speak about heaven is different from how I identify it.

3. Donald Macleod, *Jesus Is Lord: Christology Yesterday and Today* (Fearn, UK: Christian Focus Publications, 2000), 150.

4. Macleod, *Jesus Is Lord*, 3–4.

5. Grant R. Osborne, *Revelation: Verse by Verse*, Osborne New Testament Commentaries (Bellingham, WA: Lexham Press, 2016), 374.

6. J. R. R. Tolkien, *The Hobbit, or, There and Back Again* (Boston, MA; New York, NY: Houghton

Mifflin Harcourt; Mariner Books, 2012), 66.

7. I am indebted to Pastor Wayne Kinde, a great friend and mentor, for all the magnificent conversations we have had pertaining to this point and the cosmology of Genesis 1–3.

8. N. T. Wright, *Revelation for Everyone* (Louisville, KY: Westminster John Knox, 2015), 198.

9. Richard D. Phillips, Reformed Expository Commentary: *Revelation*. Philipsburg, New Jersey: P&R Publishing Company, 2017, 181.

10. See Revelation 1:10, as it was Jesus' voice in the previous verse.

11. N. T. Wright, *Revelation for Everyone* (Louisville, KY: Westminster John Knox, 2015), 42.

12. N. T. Wright, *Revelation for Everyone*, 43.

13. Cf. 1 Timothy 6:16.

14. Ronald Trail, *An Exegetical Summary of Revelation 1–11*, 2nd edition. (Dallas, TX: SIL International, 2008), 121.

15. Note that the eschatological rewards of Revelation 2–3 are a mixture of inaugurated rewards to be presently experienced *and* future rewards that will be given at the consummation of the kingdom.

16. Cf. Ezekiel 1:13; Hebrews 12:18–21.

17. And/or Zechariah 4:2.

18. Gordon D. Fee, *Revelation*, New Covenant Commentary Series (Eugene, OR: Cascade Books, 2011), 70–71.

19. Grant R. Osborne, *Colossians & Philemon: Verse by Verse*, Osborne New Testament Commentaries

(Bellingham, WA: Lexham Press, 2016), 80.

20. Richard Bauckham, *The Theology of the Book of Revelation* (Cambridge, United Kingdom: Cambridge University Press, 25th printing, 2016), 31.

21. Revelation chapters 4 and 5 are getting us ready for the arrival of the new heavens and new earth in chapters 21 and 22. But first, the apocalypse is revealing how the heavenly kingdom arrives. Revelation 4 is the stage and setting; chapter 5 is the drama.

22. The four living creatures likely represent the totality of animate creation: wild animals (lion), domesticated animals (ox), human beings (man), and birds (eagle).

23. "Holiness," edited by Douglas Mangum et al., *Lexham Theological Wordbook*, Lexham Bible Reference Series (Bellingham, WA: Lexham Press, 2014).

24. Gordon D. Fee, *Revelation*, New Covenant Commentary Series (Eugene, OR: Cascade Books, 2011), 71.

25. Anthony A. Hoekema, *The Bible and the Future* (Grand Rapids, MI; Cambridge, U.K.: William B. Eerdmans Publishing Company, 1994), 287.

26. The rewards listed may sound diverse, but they are saying basically the same thing. The context of the Church determines the reward; Jesus speaks to His people using words and rewards relevant to them. However, since Revelation 2–3 really consists of letters to the Church at large, the rewards are for any Christian from any generation.

27. Craig Blomberg, *Matthew*, vol. 22, The New

American Commentary (Nashville, TN: Broadman & Holman, 1992), 304.

28. See Galatians 4:19 and Ephesians 4:13.

29. Tom Wright, *Surprised by Hope* (London: Society for Promoting Christian Knowledge, 2007), 174.

30. For example: Genesis 1:1; Isaiah 44:24; Ephesians 3:9; and Colossians 1:16.

31. Revelation 2:7, 10; 3:5; 13:8; 17:8; 20:12, 15; 21:6, 27; 22:1, 2, 14, 17, 19.

32. Walter A. Elwell and Barry J. Beitzel, "Eternal Life," in *Baker Encyclopedia of the Bible* (Grand Rapids, MI: Baker Book House, 1988), 724; Cf. also, Ronald F. Youngblood, F. F. Bruce, and R. K. Harrison, Thomas Nelson, editors, *Nelson's New Illustrated Bible Dictionary* (Nashville, TN: Thomas Nelson, Inc., 1995).

33. A. Berkeley Mickelsen, "Eternal Life," edited by Chad Brand et al., *Holman Illustrated Bible Dictionary* (Nashville, TN: Holman Bible Publishers, 2003), 511.

34. Tom Wright, *Surprised by Hope*, 173.

35. To list a few out of the many more: Proverbs 13:14; 14:27; Jeremiah 21:8; John 3:16; 5:24; Romans 6:23; 2 Timothy 1:10; 1 John 3:14; Revelation 2:10.

36. This is where we get the subject of "biology," which is the study of natural life.

37. William Arndt et al., *A Greek-English Lexicon of the New Testament and Other Early Christian Literature* (Chicago: University of Chicago Press, 2000), 430.

38. Robert E. Van Voorst, "Life," edited by David Noel Freedman, Allen C. Myers, and Astrid B. Beck. *Eerdmans Dictionary of the Bible* (Grand Rapids, MI: W.B. Eerdmans, 2000), 809.

39. Bauckham, *The Theology of the Book of Revelation*, 48–49.

40. C. H. Spurgeon, "Spiritual Sight and Eternal Life," in *The Metropolitan Tabernacle Pulpit Sermons*, vol. 51 (London: Passmore & Alabaster, 1905), 454.

41. Daniel L. Akin. *Exalting Jesus in Revelation*, Christ-Centered Exposition, edited by David Platt, Daniel L. Akin, and Tony Merida (Nashville, TN: Holman Reference, 2016), 124.

42. This would be a helpful time to remind ourselves that the Bible's "chapters" and "verses" are later additions and were not present in the original text. While helpful for study, they can also be detrimental if we do not see the clear conjunctions and read the books of the Bible holistically.

43. Osborne, *Revelation*, 109.

44. It is possible that John would recall Isaiah 29:11, which speaks of a book that no one can read because it is sealed.

45. This is John's favorite title for Jesus as it is used twenty-eight times to communicate Christ's person and work.

46. Cf. Exodus 20.

47. Akin. *Exalting Jesus in Revelation*, 126. See also G. K. Beale, *The Book of Revelation: A Commentary on the Greek Text*. New International Greek Testament Commentary (Grand Rapids, MI; Car-

lisle, Cumbria: W.B. Eerdmans; Paternoster Press, 1999), 351–352. "[Jesus] continues to exist as a *slaughtered* Lamb; the perfect participle ἐσφαγμένον ('having been slain') expresses an abiding condition as a result of the past act of being slain."

48. Leon Morris, *Revelation: An Introduction and Commentary*, vol. 20, Tyndale New Testament Commentaries (Downers Grove, IL: InterVarsity Press, 1987), 98.

49. C. H. Spurgeon, "God's Hand at Eventide," in *The Metropolitan Tabernacle Pulpit Sermons*, vol. 58 (London: Passmore & Alabaster, 1912), 88.

50. This is probably an allusion to Zechariah 4:10.

51. Paul Gardner, *Revelation: The Compassion and Protection of Christ*, Focus on the Bible Commentary (Ross-shire, Great Britain: Christian Focus Publications, 2002), 84.

52. Samuel Rutherford. *Letters of Samuel Rutherford*, edited by Andrew A. Bonar (Edinburgh and London: Oliphant Anderson and Ferrier, 1891), 257.

53. Cf. Luke 24:51–52; Acts 1:1–11.

54. Son of David/ Son of Man/ Son of God all carry similar royal, Messianic overtones (King, Prophet, Priest), while remaining distinct in emphasis.

55. Jarl Fossum, "Son of God," edited by David Noel Freedman, *The Anchor Yale Bible Dictionary* (New York: Doubleday, 1992), 133.

56. Psalm 88:28 in the LXX (Greek Septuagint).

57. Paul J. Achtemeier. "Mark, Gospel of," edited by David Noel Freedman, *The Anchor Yale Bible Dictionary* (New York: Doubleday, 1992), 551–

552.

58. David G. Peterson, *The Acts of the Apostles*, The Pillar New Testament Commentary (Grand Rapids, MI; Nottingham, England: William B. Eerdmans Publishing Company, 2009), 431.

59. "This scene is a coronation, as becomes evident in verse 14; recalling in different language the words of Psalm 2:6: 'I have installed my king on Zion, my holy hill.'" Bob Fyall, *Daniel: A Tale of Two Cities*, Focus on the Bible Commentary (Ross-shire, Great Britain: Christian Focus Publications, 1998), 105; Cf. also, Stephen R. Miller. *Daniel*, vol. 18, The New American Commentary (Nashville, TN: Broadman & Holman, 1994), 207.

60. "In Israelite theology, Yahweh is the high God and also is portrayed as the rider on the clouds." Victor Harold Matthews, Mark W. Chavalas, and John H. Walton. *The IVP Bible Background Commentary: Old Testament*, electronic edition (Downers Grove, IL: InterVarsity Press, 2000), Daniel 7:13–14.

61. Also note that Jesus' most frequent designation for Himself was "Son of Man" (e.g., Matthew 20:28).

62. "The most compelling evidence for the messianic identification of the son of man is furnished by Christ himself. In Mark 14:61–62 he identified himself as that 'Son of Man sitting at the right hand of the Mighty One and coming on the clouds of heaven.' There is no other passage in the Old Testament to which Christ could have been referring. Furthermore, when Christ made the claim, the high priest said, 'You have heard the blasphemy' (Mark 14:64), demonstrating that Jesus was

understood to ascribe deity to himself. Young asserts, 'The employment of this title by Jesus Christ is one of the strongest evidences that He attributed Deity to Himself.'" Stephen R. Miller. *Daniel*, vol. 18, The New American Commentary (Nashville, TN: Broadman & Holman, 1994), 209.

63. Cf. "When Jesus speaks of 'the son of man coming on the clouds', he is not talking about the second coming, but, in line with the Daniel 7 text he is quoting, about his vindication after suffering. The 'coming' is an upward, not a downward, movement." Tom Wright, *Surprised by Hope* (London: Society for Promoting Christian Knowledge, 2007), 137–138.

64. From the hymn "Crown Him with Many Crowns," by M. Bridges and G. Thring.

65. Osborne, *Revelation*, 114–115.

66. As we have already said of 1 Corinthians 5:7. Cf. also Hebrews 10:12.

67. Allan A. Boesak. *Comfort and Protest: Reflections on the Apocalypse of John of Patmos* (Philadelphia: Westminster, 1987), 56–57.

68. This points us forward to a similar point made in Revelation 12:11.

69. It is important to note that, just because a Greek verb is in the perfect tense, does not give it the same significance based on aspect alone. However, the usages I have pointed out are of a similar meaning and application.

70. More will be said about what we are saved *for* in chapters 8 through 12.

71. Leon Morris, *Revelation*, 100.

235 . THE DAWN OF THE NEW CREATION

72. Robert H. Mounce, *The Book of Revelation*, revised edition, The New International Commentary on the New Testament, edited by F. F. Bruce and Gordon D. Fee (Grand Rapids: Eerdmans, 1977), 136.

73. Osborne, *Revelation*, 115.

74. Andreas J. Köstenberger, "The Deity of Christ in John's Letters and the Book of Revelation," in *The Deity of Christ*, edited by Christopher W. Morgan and Robert A. Peterson, Theology in Community (Wheaton, IL: Crossway, 2011), 167.

75. Leon Morris, *Revelation*, 102.

76. Cf. Revelation 6:16–17 explicitly, and be aware that God's judgment is a central theme in Revelation chapters 6–20.

77. Denny Burk, John G. Stackhouse, et al, *Four Views on Hell: Second Edition* (Grand Rapids, MI: Zondervan, 2016). I want to note that we must not confuse ourselves thinking that the devil's eternal destiny is the same eternal destiny for the unbeliever. It is *possible* that Satan could suffer for eternity while unbelievers are to perish. "Whether the second death is complete destruction or everlasting torment is uncertain from Revelation, although for the Devil, beast, and false prophet, it is everlasting (20:10)." Duane F. Watson, "Death, Second," edited by David Noel Freedman. *The Anchor Yale Bible Dictionary.* (New York: Doubleday, 1992), 111.

78. For more on the appearance of the post-ascended, glorified Christ, see Revelation chapters 1, 5, and 19.

79. John N. Oswal, *The Book of Isaiah, Chapters 40–*

66, The New International Commentary on the Old Testament (Grand Rapids, MI: Wm. B. Eerdmans Publishing Co., 1998), 598–599.

80. John Wesley and Charles Wesley, *The Poetical Works of John and Charles Wesley*, edited by G. Osborn, vol. 1 (London: Wesleyan-Methodist Conference Office, 1868), 106.

81. Osborne, *Revelation*, 119.

82. John Wesley and Charles Wesley, *The Poetical Works of John and Charles Wesley*, edited by G. Osborn, vol. 1 (London: Wesleyan-Methodist Conference Office, 1868), 163.

83. Osborne, *Revelation*, 339.

84. Tom Wright, *Surprised by Hope* (London: Society for Promoting Christian Knowledge, 2007), 162.

85. Hoekema, *The Bible and the Future*, 274.

86. Cf. 2 Peter 3:13.

87. "There is a qualitative distinction between the two world orders. καινός ("new") usually indicates newness in terms of quality, not time." G. K. Beale, *The Book of Revelation*, 1040.

88. Johannes Behm. "Καινός, Καινότης, Ἀνακαινίξω, Ἀνακαινόω, Ἀνακαίνωσις, Ἐγκαινίζω," edited by Gerhard Kittel, Geoffrey W. Bromiley, and Gerhard Friedrich. *Theological Dictionary of the New Testament* (Grand Rapids, MI: Eerdmans, 1964), 447.

89. Johannes Behm. "Καινός, Καινότης, Ἀνακαινίξω, Ἀνακαινόω, Ἀνακαίνωσις, Ἐγκαινίζω," 449.

90. J. Alec Motyer, *Isaiah: An Introduction and Commentary*, vol. 20, Tyndale Old Testament

Commentaries (Downers Grove, IL: InterVarsity Press, 1999), 450.

91. Cf. Luke 12:56; Acts 2:19; 1 Corinthians 8:5; Colossians 1:16, 20; Ephesians 1:10; 3:15; Hebrews 12:26 (Haggai 2:6). Also, Hermann Sasse. "Γῆ, Ἐπίγειος," edited by Gerhard Kittel, Geoffrey W. Bromiley, and Gerhard Friedrich. *Theological Dictionary of the New Testament* (Grand Rapids, MI: Eerdmans, 1964), 678.

92. Refer to chapter 1.

93. Hoekema, *The Bible and the Future*, 284.

94. C. H. Spurgeon, *Morning and Evening: Daily Readings,* December 19th Reading (London: Passmore & Alabaster, 1896).

95. Note the reference to water flowing from God's throne and the river of water of life in Revelation 21–22.

96. Cf. 1 Corinthians 10:31.

97. Anthony A. Hoekema, "Heaven: Not Just an Eternal Day Off," *Christianity Today* (June 6, 2003), http://www.christianitytoday.com/ct/2003/122/54.0.html.

98. "Heaven" can also mean the cosmos or sky; or sometimes an indirect reference to God ("Father, I have sinned against heaven and before you" [Luke 15:21]).

99. Hoekema, *The Bible and the Future*, 285.

100. Osborne, *Revelation*, 339.

101. I find it completely fascinating that Revelation personifies death and has it thrown into the "lake of fire." How do you throw death into the lake of

fire? That is beyond my comprehension, but I am glad that Jesus promises to do it.

102. Bauckham, *The Theology of the Book of Revelation*, 27.

103. Revelation 21:1 calls the "first" creation the Greek word *protos*, which is literally "first."

104. Beale, *The Book of Revelation*, 1052–1053.

105. Osborne, *Revelation*, 342.

106. C. S. Lewis. *The Last Battle* (New York: Collier Books, 1956), 168–71. I appreciate the works of Randy Alcorn for bringing this illustration to my attention.

107. Arndt et al., *A Greek-English Lexicon of the New Testament*, 117.

108. Mark J. Keown, *Philippians*, edited by H. Wayne House, W. Hall Harris III, and Andrew W. Pitts, vol. 2, Evangelical Exegetical Commentary (Bellingham, WA: Lexham Press, 2017), 280.

109. Ronald Trail, *An Exegetical Summary of 1 Corinthians 10–16*, 2nd edition (Dallas, TX: SIL International, 2008), 328.

110. Trail, *An Exegetical Summary*.

111. *Pneuma* has a wide range of meaning: e.g., spirit, breath, wind, inner life, but "spirit," pertaining to the Holy Spirit, is one of the most frequent in the New Testament, and the context usually makes it clear.

112. Tom Wright, *Surprised by Hope* (London: Society for Promoting Christian Knowledge, 2007), 168.

113. I would argue that the anarthrous substantive is

both qualitative and definite, opposing the ESV translation, which leaves it as indefinite.

114. Hoekema, *The Bible and the Future*, 274.

115. C. H. Spurgeon, "The Christian's Manifestation," in *The Metropolitan Tabernacle Pulpit Sermons*, vol. 52 (London: Passmore & Alabaster, 1906), 439–440.

116. See chapter 3.

117. Mitchell G. Reddish. "Alpha and Omega," edited by David Noel Freedman, *The Anchor Yale Bible Dictionary* (New York: Doubleday, 1992), 161.

118. Isaiah 41:4; 44:6; 48:12.

119. Motyer, *Isaiah*, 312.

120. Bauckham, *The Theology of the Book of Revelation*, 27.

121. Arndt et al., *A Greek-English Lexicon of the New Testament*, 1067.

122. Revelation 2:7, 11, 17, 26; 3:5, 12, 21.

123. Cf. Ephesians 2:11ff.

124. Cf. John 15:4; Ephesians 2:6, 7, 10, 13; Philippians 1:1; 1 Timothy 1:14; etc. The phrase "in Christ" appears ninety-one times in the ESV, and this is not including all the other phrases that speak of our union with God through the persons of the Trinity.

125. Beale, *The Book of Revelation*, 1058.

126. D. A. Carson, *The Gospel According to John*, The Pillar New Testament Commentary (Leicester, England; Grand Rapids, MI: InterVarsity Press; W.B. Eerdmans, 1991), 569.

127. Jonathan Edwards, "The Christian Pilgrim," in *Sermons and Discourses, 1730–1733*, The Works of Jonathan Edwards Series, vol. 17, edited by Mark Valeri. (New Haven, Conn: Yale UP, 1999), 437–438.

128. Raymond C. Ortlund Jr. and R. Kent Hughes, *Isaiah: God Saves Sinners*, Preaching the Word (Wheaton, IL: Crossway Books, 2005), 445.

129. Osborne, *Revelation*, 345.

130. Bauckham, *The Theology of the Book of Revelation*, 132.

131. According to Galatians 3:16, Christ is the single offspring of Abraham who would receive the promise. So, to obtain the promises and be co-heirs with Christ (Romans 8:17), you must be united to Christ.

132. Gary V. Smith. *Isaiah 1–39*, edited by E. Ray Clendenen, The New American Commentary (Nashville, TN: Broadman & Holman, 2007), 129.

133. James L. Resseguie. *The Revelation of John: A Narrative Commentary* (Grand Rapids, MI: Baker Academic, 2009), 34.

134. Richard Brooks, *The Lamb Is All the Glory*, Welwyn Commentary Series (Darlington, England: Evangelical Press, 1986), 185.

135. Dennis E. Johnson, *Triumph of the Lamb: A Commentary on Revelation* (Phillipsburg, NJ: P&R Publishing, 2001), 309.

136. David Chilton, *Paradise Restored: A Biblical Theology of Dominion* (Fort Worth: Dominion Press, 1987), 33.

137. Cf. 1 Kings 6:20; 2 Chronicles 3:8.

138. Beale says, "The figurative nature of the number is indicated by the fact that the height of the wall, 144 cubits (= about 216 feet), would be 'hopelessly out of proportion for a city some 1,500 miles high' (= 7,000,000 feet in height, if the 12,000 stadia of v 16 were taken literally)." G. K. Beale, *The Book of Revelation*, 1074.

139. Cf. Ezekiel 48:35, in which Ezekiel calls the New Jerusalem "The Lord is there."

140. N. T. Wright, *Following Jesus: Biblical Reflections on Discipleship* (London: Society for Promoting Christian Knowledge, 1994), 31.

141. Tom Wright, *Surprised by Hope* (London: Society for Promoting Christian Knowledge, 2007), 117.

142. Meredith G. Kline, *God, Heaven and Har Magedon: A Covenantal Tale of Cosmos and Telos* (Eugene, OR: Wipf & Stock Publishers, 2006), 28.

143. Cf. 1 Kings 6:19–22, 28, 30; 7:48–50.

144. Osborne, *Revelation*, 200.

145. G. K. Beale, *A New Testament Biblical Theology: The Unfolding of the Old Testament in the New* (Grand Rapids, MI: Baker Academic, 2011), 640.

146. Bruce Milne, *The Message of Heaven and Hell: Grace and Destiny*, The Bible Speaks Today (Downers Grove, IL: InterVarsity Press, 2002), 317.

147. See Exodus 33:18–23 and 34:29–35.

148. Gary V. Smith, *Isaiah 40–66*, vol. 15B, The New American Commentary (Nashville, TN: Broadman & Holman, 2009), 626.

149. I defend John, the beloved disciple, to be the author of the Gospel of John, 1–3 John, and Revelation.

150. *The Holy Bible: New Revised Standard Version* (Nashville, TN: Thomas Nelson, 1989), Tobit 13:11.

151. C. H. Spurgeon, "Christ's Joy and Ours," in *The Metropolitan Tabernacle Pulpit Sermons*, vol. 51 (London: Passmore & Alabaster, 1905), 229.

152. C. H. Spurgeon, "Resistance to Salvation," in *The Metropolitan Tabernacle Pulpit Sermons*, vol. 51, 608, italics and bold added for emphasis.

153. C. H. Spurgeon. "Life, and the Path to It," in *The Metropolitan Tabernacle Pulpit Sermons*, vol. 49 (London: Passmore & Alabaster, 1903), 19.

154. C. H. Spurgeon, "The Fruit of the Spirit: Joy," in *The Metropolitan Tabernacle Pulpit Sermons*, vol. 27 (London: Passmore & Alabaster, 1881), 77.

155. The name of the best taco shop in San Diego County, more specifically in La Jolla on Pearl Street.

156. Literally, "to make happy."

157. Chauncey Graham and James De Lancey, *God Will Trouble the Troublers of His People*, Early American Imprints, 1639–1800; No. 8356 (New York: Printed and sold by H. Gaine, at the Bible and Crown, in Hanover-Square, 1759), 23.

158. Stephen Charnock, *The Complete Works of Ste-*

phen Charnock, vol. 1 (Edinburgh; London; Dublin: James Nichol; James Nisbet and Co.; W. Robertson; G. Herbert, 1864–1866), 364–365.

159. John Flavel, *The Whole Works of the Reverend John Flavel*, vol. 2 (London; Edinburgh; Dublin: W. Baynes and Son; Waugh and Innes; M. Keene, 1820), 216.

160. "The 'living waters' are a portrayal of eternal life." Beale, *The Book of Revelation*, 1104.

161. *Holy Bible: New Living Translation* (Carol Stream, IL: Tyndale House, 2013), Psalm 36:8–9.

162. James Montgomery Boice, *Psalms 1–41: An Expositional Commentary* (Grand Rapids, MI: Baker Books, 2005), 312.

163. My translation, "bright as crystal," agrees with A. T. Robertson. *Word Pictures in the New Testament* (Nashville, TN: Broadman Press, 1933), Re 22:1.

164. The CEB translates "shining like crystal." The GNT translates "sparkling like crystal." I imagine the luminescent rivers and vegetation of Pandora from James Cameron's *Avatar* to be the closest thing I can think of to the type of beauty and radiance that is described in Revelation 21–22. However, this is just speculation, and bias, admittedly.

165. Karl Heinrich Rengstorf, "Ποταμός, Ποταμοφόρητος, Ἰορδάνης," edited by Gerhard Kittel, Geoffrey W. Bromiley, and Gerhard Friedrich. *Theological Dictionary of the New Testament* (Grand Rapids, MI: Eerdmans, 1964), 604–605.

166. *Common English Bible* (Nashville, TN: Common English Bible, 2011), Psalm 46:4.

167. Which is referenced in Acts 19:27, 35.

168. Craig A. Evans and Craig A. Bubeck, editor, *John's Gospel, Hebrews–Revelation*, First Edition, The Bible Knowledge Background Commentary (Colorado Springs, CO; Paris, ON; Eastbourne: David C Cook, 2005), 355–356.

169. *The Holy Bible: New Revised Standard Version* (Nashville, TN: Thomas Nelson, 1989), 2 Esd 8:52–54.

170. Robert Henry Charles, editor, *Pseudepigrapha of the Old Testament*, vol. 2 (Oxford: Clarendon Press, 1913), 315.

171. Rick Brannan et al., editor, *The Lexham English Septuagint* (Bellingham, WA: Lexham Press, 2012), Enoch 25:4–5.

172. Beale, *A New Testament Biblical Theology*, 935.

173. Hoekema, *The Bible and the Future*, 275.

174. Robert G. Bratcher and Howard Hatton, *A Handbook on the Revelation to John*, UBS Handbook Series (New York: United Bible Societies, 1993), 313.

175. Hermann Strathmann, "Λατρεύω, Λατρεία," edited by Gerhard Kittel, Geoffrey W. Bromiley, and Gerhard Friedrich, *Theological Dictionary of the New Testament* (Grand Rapids, MI: Eerdmans, 1964), 62.

176. On this passage referring to both, I stand in strong agreement with Beale, *The Book of Revelation*; Morris, *The Book of Revelation*; and Robert L. Thomas. *Revelation 8–22, An Exegeti-*

cal Commentary (Chicago: Moody Press, 1995).

177. This book focuses on the theology of Revelation specifically. Just because the Holy Spirit does not receive the spotlight in this book doesn't mean He is less than God. There are many great books and passages of Scripture that speak to the person and deity of the Holy Spirit.

178. Cf. John 1:18; 1 John 4:12.

179. Bauckham, *The Theology of the Book of Revelation*, 142.

180. Walter A. Elwell and Barry J. Beitzel, "Presence of God, The," *Baker Encyclopedia of the Bible* (Grand Rapids, MI: Baker Book House, 1988), 1751.

181. Second Esdras 7:98 suggests that the righteous will see the face of God after they die, when they are "glorified."

182. The Greek middle voice is used for the verb "they will see," which is why the last part of the translation is "for themselves," highlighting the intentionality behind the grammar to say that seeing God's face is for the subject's, in this case, the viewer's benefit.

183. The singular pronoun speaking of both the Father and the Son is a sort of poetic ambiguity used in Revelation to show the "oneness" (cf. John 10:30) of the two persons while there is, paradoxically, one God. This is another example of God's complex unity as described in the very robust word—trinity. For example, the latter part of Revelation 11:15 says, "The kingdom of the world has become *the kingdom* of our Lord and of his Christ, and he will reign *forever and ever.*"

Notice how the pronoun "he" at the end is a singular pronoun, but its antecedent is both the "Lord" and "Christ." I believe the grammar is intentional and suggests that both the Lord and Christ will reign.

184. For some fun pictures of space, I found this: https://www.popsci.com/best-images-outer-space.

185. Cf. Romans 8:29–30; 1 Corinthians 15:49; Colossians 3:10.

186. C. H. Spurgeon, "The Heaven of Heaven," in *The Metropolitan Tabernacle Pulpit Sermons*, vol. 14 (London: Passmore & Alabaster, 1868), 437.

187. Spurgeon, "The Heaven of Heaven," 442.

188. Cf. Exodus 28:36–38.

189. For the mark of the beast, see Revelation 14:9; 17:5; 20:4.

190. Osborne, *Revelation*, 80.

191. Brooks, *The Lamb Is All the Glory*, 195.

192. Jonathan Edwards, *The Works of Jonathan Edwards*, vol. 1 (Banner of Truth Trust, 1974), 584.

193. 4Q475, *4QRenewed Earth.* Quoted in Beale, *A New Testament Biblical Theology.*

194. We have already explored this when looking at Revelation 5, which I suggest is the coronation of Christ's kingship as He takes the throne.

195. The theme of Christ being the last Adam can be found most explicitly in Romans 5 and 1 Corinthians 15.

196. Thomas Goodwin, *The Works of Thomas Goodwin*, vol. 1 (Edinburgh: James Nichol, 1861), 510.

197. Cf. Isaiah 33:17.

198. C. H. Spurgeon, *My Sermon Notes & 4: Matthew to Revelation*, vol. 3 (Bellingham, WA: Logos Bible Software, 2009), 396.

199. Richard Sibbes, "A Glance of Heaven" in *The Complete Works of Richard Sibbes*, vol. 4, edition Alexander Balloch Grosart (Edinburgh : James Nichol ; London : James Nisbet ; Dublin : W. Robertson, 1863), 170.

200. Lewis, *The Last Battle*, 228.

201. J. I. Packer, quoted in Mark Water. *The New Encyclopedia of Christian Quotations* (Alresford, Hampshire: John Hunt Publishers Ltd, 2000), 470.

202. While not every question is answered, some of the most important are, such as: Will disease, decay, and death exist? What will become of man's relationship with God? Will those who reject God be in heaven? Will there be a physical world? And so on.

203. Brooks, *The Lamb Is All the Glory*, 189.

204. David E. Garland, *2 Corinthians*, vol. 29, The New American Commentary (Nashville, TN: Broadman & Holman, 1999), 286.

205. Garland, *2 Corinthians*, vol 29, 287.

206. Raymond C. Ortlund Jr., *Preaching the Word: Proverbs—Wisdom That Works*, edited by R. Kent Hughes (Wheaton, IL: Crossway, 2012), 86.

207. Spurgeon, "The Heaven of Heaven," 433.

About the Author

As the Head of Publishing for Sermon To Book and Speak It To Book, Brayden is incredibly passionate about producing books that bless humanity. He loves serving the Church with his gifts, which include teaching the Bible with a refreshing combination of depth and enthusiasm. This comes from a distinctive approach to rigorous study, as evidenced by his personal library of over 12,000 books. He is a life-long learner of all things theological and is especially interested in further advanced study in biblical Greek.

Brayden is launching a podcast (The Rooted Podcast), and beginning the preliminary stages of his next book. His fervent goal is to show how the grand narrative of the Bible is the most exciting and worthy story of all time—and how the gospel invites us to participate in this greatest story through relationship with Jesus.

You can contact Brayden via email (brayden@speakittobook.com) to share how his book has blessed you, talk about publishing, or invite him to speak at your event. Brayden lives in San Diego, California, with his wife, Ariana.

About Sermon To Book

SermonToBook.com began with a simple belief: that sermons should be touching lives, *not* collecting dust. That's why we turn sermons into high-quality books that are accessible to people all over the globe.

Turning your sermon series into a book exposes more people to God's Word, better equips you for counseling, accelerates future sermon prep, adds credibility to your ministry, and even helps make ends meet during tight times.

John 21:25 tells us that the world itself couldn't contain the books that would be written about the work of Jesus Christ. Our mission is to try anyway. Because in heaven, there will no longer be a need for sermons or books. Our time is now.

If God so leads you, we'd love to work with you on your sermon or sermon series.

Visit www.sermontobook.com to learn more.

Made in the USA
Columbia, SC
24 August 2019